How to prevent Suicide

Gilda Rodriguez

ISBN: 979-8-8691-6963-1

Contents

Dedication

To all my family and friends.

My book is for every person who likes to know about problems related to suicide and need to find a solution and conclusion to a problem depending the issue.

Made with love and respect, this book is for you.

Acknowledgment

To all teens and people who have problems and have thought about suicide

About the Author

I am a graduate student from the University of Phoenix in San Diego, California. I enjoy reading and sharing my thoughts with people who like to hear the other side of the story.

Despite everything, I love life.

High Suicide Rates

We live in a contemporary society where almost all kinds of people, genders, and cliques are welcomed. The keyword here is almost.

As we inch towards a more accepting society, it must be noted that this move is prolonged and gradual. The truth is bullies walk among us at large. They openly attack those who are vulnerable and make crude jokes at their expense. Thus, it is no surprise that suicide rates among teenagers and young adults have skyrocketed over the last few years.

Suicide is one of the biggest contributors to early death in America. According to research, it is one of the top 3 leading reasons behind the mortality rate in the United States for people within the 10-34-year-old age bracket. It was also reported that for every young person that successfully commits suicide, there are thousands who attempt it.

Not only is this alarming news, but it is rather scary. If we do not take steps to reduce and eliminate this, things can go horribly wrong in the future. If this keeps up, we will inevitably lose thousands of people from the younger generation to suicide.

The statistics are usually different for everyone based on various factors such as age and gender. For the purpose of this book, it must be noted that cliques that represent minorities are high up on the list of those who commit, attempt, or even contemplate suicide.

Life Advice for Teenagers

Teenage is a difficult time. Many people struggle to survive that period of their lives. But when you look back at your life, most of us have plenty of advice for our younger selves.

Here are a few pieces of advice I have for you because I was a teenager not too long ago.

• You must be wise and strong-headed.

• Do not let other people influence you.

• Be mindful.

• Be positive.

• Do not let anyone peer-pressure you. You make your own choices and decisions.

• Do not say 'yes' when you want to say 'no.'

• Set boundaries early on, even if they make you a jerk.

• Think over your decisions – do not act impulsively. Living in the moment sounds fun until you make a mistake and spend the next five years of your life correcting that mistake and regretting your spontaneous decision.

• Be confident about yourself, and never let anyone put you down.

• Don't follow trends and trendsetters: be yourself.

• If you are bullied, put a stop to it no matter what.

• Speak up! Do not suppress your thoughts.

• Avoid mindless surfing on the internet – especially when it comes to dark subjects.

• Be careful with drugs. Getting involved with drugs early on may make you look 'cool,' but it will only mess up your life in the long run.

• Think of the bigger picture; always look at the long-term plan of it all.

Now, it is no secret that the suicide rate among teenagers is increasing. However, during studies, researchers have categorized teenagers based on their music preferences. Obviously, music is something they are consuming all the time.

The studies showed an association between being a heavy metal fan and suicidal risk. Researchers also identified people who self-harm are associated with the same lifestyle as that of an Emo person.

Emo (short for emotional) is a sub-culture and clique many people – especially youngsters- fit into. As the name suggests, members are emotional people. But there's more to it, isn't there?

Emos are people who identify themselves as outsiders – they look at the world from the perspective of an outsider. Not only that, they make sure that their appearance is that of an outsider. They tend to wear black clothes (Preferred clothes: skinny jeans, band tees, wristbands, studded belts). They are usually adorned with dark eye makeup and typically have bangs and dyed hair.

Furthermore, they love isolating themselves. They are willing to go to extreme lengths to isolate themselves. For instance, they listen to loud music to keep their distance from people. Hate those around them and themselves, have lost all hope. They deal with life with a pessimistic attitude and would prefer not to exist.

Moreover, they absolutely love the idea of death and always have to mention their depression. Once they constantly surround themselves with a depressive environment, they are more likely to have suicidal tendencies.

Emos usually come from broken families or abusive households. Considering that they have so much in life, it is understood that this group of people emanates sadness. Unfortunately, most people fail to see or understand where they are coming from.

In fact, they go as far as to bully them. The combination of bullies and emos is deadly. While an emo person wants to loudly express their emotions, a bully would never realize where these emotions are coming from. They would never realize that their ignorant attitude can have severe consequences.

An emo person, all while dealing with their own problems, usually adds more problems to their life through their lifestyle. While screaming out your emotions is healthy, it is never okay to display each thought to everyone. Some things, like their need to die, should be kept under wraps and must always be shared with people who genuinely care. When they are trying to display their emotions, they must also realize that not everyone is as empathic. Not everyone will understand. This, in turn, only furthers their self-hatred and ignites their self-esteem issues.

An emo person has already surrounded themselves with hate. They don't further need it from other people. However, when more hate is thrown at them, it only adds to their suicidal tendencies.

This is why I believe we have failed collectively as a society. We must work together to prevent suicide because every life matters! Let us join hands and ensure we will play our part in suicide prevention!

Thoughts For Emo-Influenced Teens

The first step is realizing just how harmful suicide is. Not only will it impact you, but it will also hurt those around you. If that still doesn't give you a reason to stop, then do it for yourself. Once you stumble over this realization and pledge to eliminate all your suicidal thoughts, you are ready for the next step.

Here are a few tips that you can follow that will help you:

• Wake up early and meditate.

• Read the Bible for a good start to the day.

• Try to feel God's presence: know that He is always with you in good ways, even when it doesn't feel like it.

• Start your day with positive affirmations. Tell yourself that "Today will be a blessed and happy day" and "I am worth it. I deserve to be here. I deserve to have a good day."

• Avoid thinking you must listen to sad songs or write sad poetry to fit in with your social circle or other friends. Instead, try to have positive thoughts.

• Spend your time doing productive things to keep your mind busy.

• Fix yourself a healthy lunch every day. Try incorporating vegetables and fruits into your diet.

• Look for things that you are grateful for and list them down.

• Try journalling but give a positive spin to it!

• Try avoiding negative people and talk.

• Do not indulge in conversations that promote self-harm or suicide.

• Practice mindfulness meditation to ensure that you put a cap on all negative thoughts and feelings.

The Problematic Lifestyle of Emos

It is no secret that depression mainly occurs from the negativity we surround ourselves with. Our brain processes about 70,000 thoughts every day. If most of these thoughts are negative, they will subconsciously impact our decisions. Causing us to act out in many different ways.

While Emos articulate their emotions through poetry, like most of their thoughts, poetry is also harmful. It is filled with negativity. Life can be difficult, and we will always find numerous people who are hell-bent on bringing us down. Expressing such emotions in your poetry will make you feel released and become a better person. And if it does, please continue to write.

Sometimes, it is healthy to take out your emotions, but not in every situation. Let's take an example of it.

Trees are known to have a life span of 600 or more years. However, according to research, if you go up to a tree and launch negative comments on it every single day, it will eventually die, even before its life expectancy.

In trying times or in depression, what humans crave is a connection. Now it could be with a friend, partner, pet, or parent. Emos are people too. No matter how much they would argue against it, they need someone in their lives. Someone with whom they could share their dreams or perhaps their fears. And there's nothing wrong with that.

However, we fail to focus on the most critical connection with anyone. Our relationship with God. God is going to provide you with the comfort you need. He is going to guide you throughout your life. God will never leave your side.

Thus, when you wake up in the morning, read the Bible. Remind yourself that today will be a blessed and happy day. Avoid the need to write sad poetry to fit in with your social group. Instead, focus on having positive thoughts.

Another problem attached to the Emo lifestyle is the excessive use of drugs. Emos are usually bullied. Thus, in search of solitude, they turn to drugs. Let me tell you that is never the answer to any problem. Drugs may temporarily solve your problems, but once they become a part of your life, they will be the main cause behind all the issues in your life.

It takes no time to become addicted to drugs; once you do, you lose your sanity, your life, and everyone around it. The usage of drugs is also very common in the Emo teen lifestyle. It is also one of the main causes of the increasing suicide rates.

Drugs may help you escape reality, but it takes you so far from it that, at a time, nothing makes sense without them. That is a state of insanity. Not only do you lose your own life, but you lose your friends, family, and other beloved relations.

If you realize that you are addicted to drugs, it is advised to seek professional help. Get yourself checked by a specialist, or check into rehab for a better lifestyle.

If you feel like you are being pressured to take drugs, get yourself as far away from those people as possible. Don't fall into the dark pit with them. Open your eyes and consider the negative aspects of it.

As mentioned above, appearance matters the most for an Emo lifestyle. While their clothes are black, one aspect of their clothing is that all of it is skinny. As a result of this, emos often find themselves trying to fit into the skinny appearance. They want to be the skinniest person on the planet so they can wear skinny and tight clothes.

This behavior results in eating disorders, especially for people with curvy bodies. Teenagers are often bullied about their appearance, causing them to resort to harming themselves. They don't realize the effects of this on their physical and mental health. To add salt to their wounds, if they resort to dressing up as Emo, they are putting themselves in a harmful situation.

Emos are almost never accepted by society. They are ridiculed and made to feel like outcasts. Once these feelings get ingrained in the minds of a teenager, their suicidal tendencies are going to win. At first, they will begin to consider themselves unworthy and talk down on themselves. Then, they will resort to ways to harm themselves and, eventually, will do suicide.

Cutting yourself may seem like the only solution to this problem, but they fail to realize that they are made perfect just the way they are. You don't need to fit into the perception society has made for you. Instead, you should focus your energy on being healthy. That is what matters the most. Your body is a blessing from God. You should be able to utilize it.

Yet if you still don't feel comfortable in your body, try to work out and get in your desired shape. There are healthy ways to diet and keep your body active.

Emos also often fall into habits of witchcraft which I believe comes due to their beliefs. Emos believe they don't have a God. Their appearance is what represents their belief. Thus, they switch to witch crafting and have dark bibles, which they use to hunt people for protection.

This only comes from the lack of faith in God. Since their lives have been terrible, they believe that God doesn't exist. However, they must realize that this is not the case. God is always there for you. They should once open the Bible and read its message. Only then will they understand the true meaning of Christianity.

Considering all the issues above, I believe the main cause of this problem is the media. It plays a huge role in influencing young people's minds. The media, through rockstars and celebrities, is the one that displayed Emo as cool.

Marilyn Manson can be considered one of the representatives of emo society. Her chemical romance, emo metal bands, local punks, and goths have influenced not only the music but also the fashion. Teenagers look up to people like this and consider them idols.

However, any sensible person and most teenagers would agree that this kind of fashion is strange. They only choose to act on such behaviors when they need attention or they are finding difficulties in solving their problems.

Parents whose children are going through their teenage years should always be available to help. They should be very open to their children about the inevitable problems they will face in their lives so they don't feel ashamed asking for help. Who knows, you might prevent them from taking their own life.

Signs of suicidal behavior include:

• Talking about wanting to die or to kill oneself.

• Looking for a way to kill oneself, such as searching online or obtaining a gun.

• Talking about feeling hopeless or having no reason to live.

• Talking about being a burden to others.

• Increasing the use of alcohol or drugs.

• Acting anxious or agitated; behaving recklessly.

• Sleeping too little or too much.

• Withdrawing or feeling isolated.

• Showing rage or talking about seeking revenge.

• Displaying extreme mood swings.

Suicide can be prevented with help and therapy. Seek a therapist and figure out the problem's root cause. Oftentimes, we are pushing back the real problem without realizing its impact on our physical and mental health. Also, seeking a dark lifestyle like this is only going to cause more problems in your life. It may seem like your problems are going away, but it is only temporary. Those same issues are going to keep coming back, stronger than before, if you don't face them head-on.

The Problems & Solutions

Dark Clothes

Problem

More and More emos are committing suicide because they wear dark-colored clothes and get bullied for it. They cannot handle the way they are treated and ridiculed, so they decide to give up on their lives.

Solution

This is a serious cause of concern as to why people feel that they have no other option but to take their lives and end them prematurely. Instead of committing suicide, emos should look for other solutions, such as what they can do to change or fix the problem at hand. One way to do this would be to switch up their style.

If you are an emo who is bullied for wearing the same kinds of clothes, try doing these things instead:

1. Predictability is boring; try wearing different kinds of clothes.

2. It's okay to love black and wear it, too. Just try to avoid wearing all-black outfits.

3. Add a splash of color here and there in your outfits. Try wearing colorful accessories such as shoes, bags, or belts to add that pop of color to your life.

4. Ignore your bullies, and don't let them get to you. You didn't come into this world to please them.

5. If it's possible, stand up to your bullies. Show them that you aren't scared of them or their mean jokes. When they

realize how little you care, they will move on to find someone else to bother and annoy.

Conclusion

With the passage of time, bullying has become increasingly common. It's not okay. Do not allow your bullies to bother you. Their voice does not matter. Their crude jokes aren't funny. They just make fun of you for being different because they are jealous of you. You are better than them, and they know it. They cannot stand it. So, don't let them belittle you or dampen your spirits. Next time they make fun of you, laugh at them!

Lack of Faith

Problem

There has been a rise in suicide rates amongst teens, especially in emos. One of the biggest reasons this happens is their lack of faith. When you don't have faith in God, you do not believe in His powers and supremacy. This makes it easier for you to get depressed and lose all hope. And when that happens, your suffering is inevitable. As these miseries seem to pile on top of one another, people tend to give up. They lose their will to live and end up killing themselves.

Solution

Not everyone is religious or believes in a Higher Being. However, Jesus Christ is our true savior, and we must devote ourselves to Him so that he blesses us with His infinite blessings. It is not easy to find Jesus and see the truth in His path, but once you go there, you will find a sense of peace unlike any other. It will be unparalleled to all that you have ever known or are familiar with.

Here are a few things you can try to slowly transition and move towards being a better Christian:

1. Try to read the Bible every day

2. Don't just read the Bible but also understand the word of our Lord. Go deeper than the layer of words and try to understand the interpretation of it all.

3. Try meditation – especially when you're going through hard times or feel depressed.

4. Write down verses of the Bible that seem to resonate with you the most. Place them somewhere you can see them every day. Then, read them daily and memorize them.

5. Repent and repeat. Ask God for forgiveness for the sins you have committed knowingly and unknowingly, both.

6. Try going to church as frequently as you can and try practicing what is preached.

7. Build a community. Connect with believers and people who are devoted to God and His cause. Share your thoughts and ideas with them. Watch and observe their way of life and connect with them spiritually and physically.

8. Pray as often as you can – for anything and everything that comes to your mind. Pray for the big things in life – such as living to fulfill your dreams and turning them into reality. Pray for the little things, such as having a good day or week.

9. Stay true to God. Be committed. Do not waver from the path.

10. Apply the word of God in your life through all your deeds.

Conclusion

In this modern world, most people tend to overlook or neglect faith altogether. There are those who abandon religion and give up on the belief that there is someone out there who is Sovereign and above all their worldly issues. And when that happens, it gets easier to forget our purpose in life. It is easier to go astray. This is the reason why there is so much hurt, pain, and chaos in our world today. We must do what we can to put an end to all this misery and suffering. And the only way to do this is to allow Jesus back in your life and to let Him show you the right path.

Depression

Problem

There has been a steady rise in suicide rates among teens. Suicide rates have especially skyrocketed in emos, and one of the leading factors behind this is that emos are generally depressed. It is wrong to generalize and classify a vast group of people into one single category. However, the best way to describe teenagers today is to call them depressed.

What is depression? It is a shadow of misery and sadness cast over your life. It looms over you and threatens to affect all that you are. Everything you do and every single thought that you have is easily affected and impacted by this cloud of depression. It negatively impacts you to the point that it can even prove to be lethal.

Solution

It's not easy to keep a cap on your thoughts, especially when they are so dark, depressive, and consuming. So, how exactly do you contain such thoughts? How do you move past this overwhelmingly uncontrollable sadness and move on to a place that makes you feel better? How do you cut back on all the negative energy and feel happy? How do you negate the negativity and embrace positivity instead?

Well, there are a few things that you can try that will help you move past these feelings of desolation and grief:

1. The first thing that you can do to keep the depression at bay is to try mindfulness. Mindful meditation is a great way to try and control your thoughts. When you feel drawn in by

negative energy or thoughts, try to divert your attention and focus on mindful meditation instead. There are many mindfulness meditation exercises available online that will help you keep negative thoughts away from your mind. This will help ensure that negative energy does not eat you away and claim you whole.

2. Find happiness in the little things in life. Instead of getting upset over things like rain or snow, look at the brighter side of the picture. Find meaning and happiness in whatever is happening in your life. Find the silver lining in the dark cloud of depression that looms over your life.

3. Find meaning in your living. Try to be there for other people. Little acts of service can make you feel better; they fill you with a feeling of contentment unparalleled to all other feelings in the world. Help others through your words or actions, and let it fulfill you.

4. Learn to keep yourself busy. When you are idle, it is easier for you to get consumed by overwhelming negative thoughts. This can be quite a disaster, especially when you're already battling depression. In such cases, it is better to keep yourself occupied and busy so that your brain doesn't get the time to come up with negative thoughts and ideas that can dampen your mood and spirit.

5. Live in the present. You must focus on where you are and enjoy the moment as it is. Live in the present, and don't worry too much about the past or the future. You need to know that what matters the most is the present and devote all your thoughts to it.

6. Exercise and eat clean. This may sound unrelated, but studies have proven that these two things have a direct and positive impact on uplifting your spirits. So, avoid eating junk food and unhealthy snacks. You don't necessarily have to go on a diet but try incorporating more greens into your diet, and you will notice a difference yourself!

7. Focus on relationships and people that make you feel better. Certain people make life seem easier; stick to them; keep them close to your heart. Unfortunately, there are also people in this world who make life difficult. They are toxic and seem to drain out all your energy. Cut them off! There is no use in keeping up with a relationship that only takes and takes from you.

8. Avoid drugs when you are battling depression. I know that most people tend to turn towards drugs, be it joints, pills, or drinks, but the truth – that most people don't know is – that these drugs actually mess up your emotional balance more than they fix them. They create an imbalance in your emotions, leading to extreme mood swings. Moreover, they are also harmful and addictive. So, it is best to avoid them as best as possible.

9. Refer back to the previous section. Ultimately, God is the only solution to all your problems. Turn to Him; find peace and healing in His words. Let Him and His scripture heal you and guide you on the right path.

10. If things still seem to spiral out of control and don't seem to get better, you should seek professional help. Consult a therapist or psychologist and let them help you.

Conclusion

Depression is no joke – and it shouldn't be treated as such. Depression is the biggest reason why people commit suicide. It can eat you away slowly but surely. It takes a negative toll on your being and can be quite difficult to control. Try to keep your negative thoughts at bay; try to elude the sadness from your life.

The Attitude

Problem

One of the biggest problems with the emo culture is their attitude. The issue with emos is that they like to glamorize pain and suffering. They are so obsessed with depression and death that they look over these morbid things with fascination. Emos often get bullied because their attitude bothers other people. To people, they are troubled people and very proud of it. They believe there is nothing wrong with being unhappy and casting a shadow of darkness and gloom on others. For this reason, they get bullied by other people who don't feel the same way as they do. And sometimes, when the bullying gets too much, emos feel that there is no other option but to give up. That's when they make the decision to take their lives.

Solution

While depression is a real crisis, the one thing that actually adds to it and even prevents a person from healing is attitude. If you take on the "I am fine the way I am" attitude, you will only add to your suffering.

Emos often consider a list of questions: How to avoid bullying? How to make our lives better? How to put an end to all this misery and pain?

If these questions sound familiar – or if any of the above things resonate with you, here's a list of things you can do:

1. The first thing that you need to do is to realize that life is a journey of constant progress. You cannot just sit in a state

of stagnancy. The first step is to embrace this mindset. Understand that you need to keep moving forward. If you're depressed, you can't just think that it's okay to be depressed for the rest of your life. There will be happy days; know that and work for that.

2. This brings me to the next point. Know that it will require you to put in the effort and hard work to save yourself. What does this mean? Simply put, life isn't a movie. There's no knight in shining armor or man on a white horse that will save you. Only you can save yourself. And it will happen if you work on improving yourself.

3. Try to stop thinking that where you are currently in your life is the ideal place for you to be at. As discussed, progress is necessary and constant in life, so always strive to be the best version of yourself. Constant improvement is the way to live! Do not sit back and take a backseat role in your life simply because you enjoy misery and want to stay in a dark place.

4. Self-awareness is the next important plan. Know yourself. What are the things that you want to improve about yourself? What are the things that you wish were different? What do you think can be improved to give you a better quality of life? Contemplate over these questions and be honest with your answers. Remember the points previously discussed when answering these questions.

5. Make a plan and take action. Have a vision board. Where do you stand right now? Where do you want to be 3 or 6 months from now? How do you plan on achieving that? Write down your long-term goals. Break it down into

smaller, bite-sized goals that are easier for you to achieve. Next, work on achieving these milestones so you eventually hit the more significant milestones in life – the way you have planned and intended for yourself.

6. Find your purpose in life and try to live it. Do things that fill you with happiness and contentment. It must be noted that these things shouldn't include activities like self-harming or drugs.

7. Keep yourself engaged in activities that promote self-growth.

8. Continue to reflect and grow.

Conclusion

With the passage of time, bullying has become increasingly common. While it's easier to blame others for being horrible and inconsiderate people, sometimes, things happen in our favor. The only problem is that, more often than not, we do not realize that things are happening FOR us, not to us. Sometimes, we get bullied for things that we should improve. We should always try to take a positive approach to life and try to look at the bigger picture.

Self-Harm

Problem

There has been a rise in suicide rates amongst teens, especially in emos. One of the biggest reasons this happens is because they are so involved in self-harm. Most emos like to cut themselves or hurt themselves in other ways, including burning themselves. Sometimes, they take it too far and end up committing suicide.

It is easy to be upset and blame the world for your problems. But taking action against it in the form of self-harm is wrong and simply unacceptable. Do not glorify self-harm; there is nothing good about it.

Solution

To put it simply, the only solution to this problem is to stop harming yourself. Don't hurt yourself. Just because you're in pain emotionally or mentally does not mean that you have to put your physical being at risk as well. Of course, it's easier said than done. And so, I am sharing a list of things that you can do to avoid self-harm:

1. The first step is always realization. Know that self-harm is wrong; the scars that you wear on your skin are reminders of the pain you have inflicted on yourself. Just because other people have hurt you does not mean that you will hurt yourself too. The sooner you realize this, the quicker you will stop. Because after you realize that it is wrong, you must prepare yourself for the next step: putting an end to it.

2. Put a curb to your suicidal or harmful thoughts. It's easy to think about hurting yourself when it has been your answer to things for a long time. But it is important to realize that you must not fall back on the same destructive path. Direct your thoughts towards something positive, and convert the negative energy you are feeling in the moment you want to harm yourself to someone else.

3. Think of it as a habit and work towards breaking it. It takes 21 days to form a habit and the same amount of time to break it.

4. Discipline yourself! Learn to control your thoughts.

5. Mindfulness meditation is always a great way to put a lid on all your negative feelings and destructive thoughts. Mindfulness allows you to focus on the present moment. When you're upset, you tend to make rash decisions. When you practice mindfulness meditation, you take a step back and slow down. You allow your mind and body to calm down and let go of the burdens that are holding you back. Through simple and easy exercises, you are able to focus on the present moment. It is a great way to stop yourself from hurting yourself.

6. When you feel as though the world has let you down, you must understand that this is the way things are in this life. What you need to focus on is God and His love. Turn to Jesus Christ, as He is the only answer to all your problems. Everyone in this world can let you down but never Him!

7. Seek professional help. It is obvious that you have a troubled life that is burdening you and impacting the way

you live. Talk to people, and take the help that you need to move past this destructive coping mechanism.

Conclusion

Most people like to hurt themselves when they go through circumstances that hurt them. When asked why they self-harm, many people will answer that they want to turn the focus of their emotional suffering to physical pain – something that is still easier for them to bear and live with.

The Us Versus Them Mentality

Problem

There are so many people in this world, and it is only normal for everyone to be different and unique. It is expected for individuals to be different and behave differently. Owing to the fact that human beings are social creatures, they tend to stick with one another.

While this isn't necessarily a bad thing, it must be noted that it has given rise to the clique culture. We like to put labels on people to define them. Sooner or later, this is how bullying seeps in.

Solution

If you look at the social structure of a high school, you will find many cliques: the popular crowd, jocks, cheerleaders, nerds, goths, emos, anime or manga fans, druggies and stoners, and so on and so forth. Sometimes, this may include different ethnic groups as well, especially minorities.

All of these groups exist together, but the challenge is sometimes, they don't know how to peacefully coexist together. This is mostly because everyone has the 'us versus them' mentality. Everyone looks down on anyone who isn't them. We like to believe that we are better than others, and so we belittle others. We have this superiority complex where we judge others. Sometimes, we do this secretly and are quiet about it. Other times, we can be quite vocal about this.

This can create a lot of unnecessary hatred and drama. In turn, this gives rise to competition and rivalry. This may even start dirty politics and problems that can easily be avoided if we skip this mentality.

Hatred and suspicion can create a divide between all cliques. This gives rise to bullying in various different forms. While bullying itself is wrong, here are a few things that we can do to try and bridge this gap:

1. Try to be friendly to everyone around you. Treat people the way you want to be treated.

2. If you are suspicious or wary, others will be, too. Suspicion breeds suspicion – and it's the same way for any other emotion. If you want people to be nice to you, you must be nice to them as well.

3. Be kind even when others aren't.

4. Don't do something only to expect something else in return. Don't depend on other people. Keep your expectations low.

5. Be helpful but know when to draw a line between nice and naïve.

6. Don't hold onto negativity. Try to extend a helping hand or an olive branch when you can. There's already enough negative energy in this world. You should focus on reducing it as opposed t adding more to it.

7. Stop separating yourself from others. At the end of the day, God created us all as equals. Remember: no one is better than the other, and we're all the same!

8. Don't look down on other people. Don't be judgemental. Be more accepting of other people and their differences. It's okay to have differing opinions – but it is not okay to make fun of people for that reason.

Conclusion

God didn't create us as different people and placed us in this world just so we could highlight each other's differences and ridicule one another. He did this so that we could each serve our unique purpose in life. God does not encourage a divide between His people. Therefore, instead of focusing on how we are different, we should find similarities and common grounds with one another to bridge the gap we have created ourselves.

They are Disturbed

Problem

The harsh reach of life spares no man and soul. Everyone suffers through something or the other in the walk of life. It is simply the way things are. Trauma is part and parcel of life – and it always leaves a scar. However, everyone reacts differently to trauma. Some people manage to hide and mask their scars. Others allow them to heal and are able to recover from it. But not everyone is fortunate enough to do so.

Trauma tends to cut deep. It hurts and devastates people. It alters who they are and changes their perspective. Some people take that pain in their lives and sit with it, feeding it and allowing it to grow bigger and bigger – until it becomes unmanageable for them. Their pain controls their life because it is a beast that they cannot control or tame.

This is usually the case with emos. They have seen such difficulties and suffered so much in life that they don't know how to move past their trauma. They are chained and imprisoned to their worst memories, and try as they might, they cannot move on from it.

The problem that makes most emos commit suicide and even harm themselves – and sometimes, those around them, is that they are disturbed. And the everyday occurrences of life only add to their pain. There is nothing that saves them from this pain. There is no mercy and no escape for them.

Solution

I am sharing a list of things that you can do to avoid self-harm. While I understand that life may be difficult and there are days where ending it feels like the only solution, trust me when I say this, suicide is not the answer. You have seen the worst in life. Now, you should be brave and stick around for the good part.

1. Know that you need help and seek it from those around you. Take help from family and friends. Learn to trust them and reveal what you feel about them.

2. If talking to trusted people doesn't help, reevaluate who you trust. If the people you open up to are part of the problem, know that it is time for you to change your support system.

3. If none of these tips help you, I would strongly advise seeking professional help. Talk to a counselor or a therapist; it might help direct your thoughts and help you realize where you are coming from.

4. Put a curb to your suicidal or harmful thoughts. Direct your thoughts towards something positive, and convert the negative energy you are feeling in the moment you want to harm yourself to something else – something that is useful and productive.

5. Don't wallow in self-pity or misery. Change your attitude from 'woe is me' and try to look for the lessons that life is trying to teach you.

6. When you feel as though the world has let you down, you must understand that this is the way things are in this life.

What you need to focus on is God and His love. Turn to Jesus Christ, as He is the only answer to all your problems, even if you don't feel that way because you are disturbed right now. Everyone in this world can let you down but never Him! Remember that God will never put you through more than what you cannot endure.

Conclusion

Pain is a part of life – and that's all it is. Nothing more and nothing less. Do not let your pain control you and who you are. Know that your life matters more than the pain – even if it seems impossible at that moment. There is no shame in seeking help, so do not shy away from it!

Extremely Sensitive

Problem

There are so many people in this world, and yet, every single person in this world is different and unique. We react to things differently. Some people are strong and can endure the worst storms of their lives with a smile on their faces. Other people are sensitive and tend to break down easily in the face of hardships.

Don't worry about this. Don't think that this is a bad thing. The truth is that we are all unique. It doesn't matter if we are wired differently. What matters is not who we were when we came into this world but rather, who we become, when we leave this world.

So, when the time comes, who do you want to be? Do you want to be the person who cries and quits in the face of difficulties? Or do you want to be the person who deals with their problems boldly and bravely?

Solution

Building personality and working on yourself is crucial. In this world and life, you will only succeed if you constantly focus on self-growth and self-improvement. Work on yourself and your development each day, and focus on being a better and improved version of yourself each day.

Here are a few ways to work on yourself:

1. Know that life is hard – that things are bound to be difficult. Once you acknowledge that, you will be at ease. You will not stress or despair about life.

2. Don't let your fear chain you. I know that fear can be a scary thing and that it may hold you down and impede your growth. But I want you to know that fear is just an emotion. It is simply a thought that scares you. Let go of that fear, and you will find yourself winning in life.

3. Find someone you can look up to – a mentor or someone who will help you grow and become the best version of yourself. Stick to them and take in their advice. Observe and mimick them.

4. Work on improving your self-esteem. Be confident!

5. Find your purpose, set goals, and reach them. Setting targets and accomplishing them will make you brave.

6. Increase your self-awareness. Know your strengths and weaknesses. Next, work on improving everything about yourself.

7. Don't be too hard on yourself! People make mistakes – learn and accept them.

Conclusion

God didn't create us as different people and placed us in this world just so we would remain the same way. He created us differently so that we may bring out the best in others – pick up the best from other people and show our best for other people to learn from us. So, let's focus on doing that!

Drugs

Problem

When presented with a problem, we often look for quick solutions that will bring about quick changes and help solve our problem. More often than not, drugs are taken as a solution to the problem at hand. Drugs help divert attention. They are not solutions. However, people think that they help with the situation. The consumption of drugs has experienced a growing trend recently. To add fuel to this already blazing fire, the easy accessibility of drugs also contributes to it.

There is a common misconception about what the consumption of drugs can lead to. People think of it as an easy getaway or escape from reality. However, that is not the case. In most cases, it leads to bad decisions being made when you're under the influence. Hence, after sobering up, regret follows. When people find themselves in a mess, they cannot see an easy way out of it; they choose to commit suicide.

Solution

I am sharing a list of things that need to be realized by every individual currently using or considering using drugs. Realizing what you're about to do is important, as no decisions should be made without weighing them out.

It is not a solution to your problems.

1. It is not an escape from reality.

2. It will not help you make better decisions.

3. It leads to a deteriorating lifestyle.

4. It is not healthy.

5. Regret will follow.

6. No matter how bad a situation might get, suicide is not the answer.

Addiction can lead to an individual being stuck in a ritualistic cycle, where he cannot stop consuming drugs and struggles with an imbalance of hormones, leading to irregular emotions being experienced. This can eventually lead to dark thoughts entering your mind. People often look for a way out- suicide. People are scared of joining rehabilitation centers and changing their lifestyle, not understanding that if they continue to live the way their living, they will develop multiple medical disorders that will add to their agony.

This is more of a problem in teens than in any other age demographic because drugs have been presented as something "the cool kids" use. This false portrayal of drugs is detrimental to societies. The kids start consuming drugs, unaware of how easy it is to develop an addiction, only to realize when it's too late.

The first step is always the most difficult to take. It's an uncomfortable but important one. The first step is to decide to stop using drugs and make a change. Next, if you fail to do it on your own, don't be afraid to reach out to a sibling or a parent. There is nothing to be ashamed of. We're all humans and could do with a little support every now and then. If the person you contacted cannot help, reach out to a therapist and a rehab facility and seek treatment.

Conclusion

God has blessed us with a beautiful body and complete control over it. Without you being in control, it serves no purpose and will lead to bad decisions. A ship is nothing without its captain. Likewise, your body is nothing without you taking complete control of it. Our problems can only be sorted by putting out minds to it. Administering substances will not help us deal with our issues.

Broken Families

Problem

Your surrounding leaves a huge impact on you. The energy you are surrounded with is what trains your mind. Often, families do not realize this fact. A house with little to no communication can lead to a drastic impact on an individual. Family is where you're supposed to be allowed to be the most vulnerable. So, when an individual is not allowed to do that, they start bottling up emotions that lead to an unstable balance. Once you're not allowed to express your emotions freely, you start feeling left out and eventually start looking for a solution. When at their worst, without a place to look for an answer, they commit suicide.

Solution

As big as this problem might look, it is easily avoidable if the people involved are willing to take the necessary steps.

• The first is to utilize the most overlooked tool that can be used to solve such issues, communication. Communication is key to tackling such issues as an individual can express his feelings, compared to bottling them up when there is little to no communication.

• The next step is for every family member to examine and analyze themselves. Then they should decide how they can improve.

• It is also necessary that bonding exercises are practiced ritualistically. Family dinners, picnics, and movie nights are examples of exercises that are sure to help.

• Be open to criticism. Everyone in the family should keep an open mind and give others the benefit of the doubt. They should understand that a family is the closest friend they can have, and there must be trust that should be developed.

Conclusion

The importance of family needs to be understood by every individual. They are your best friends and will always want what's best for you. Every family should keep its dynamic in check. Energy must surround everyone, which will help all members thrive and grow.

Their Trauma

Problem

A dreadful event in life, such as an accident, being raped, or a natural disaster, can cause an emotional response known as trauma. Shock and denial are common responses in the moments immediately following an occurrence. In the longer term, effects can include unpredictable emotions, memories, strained relationships, and even physical problems such as headaches or nausea. Despite the fact that these emotions are quite natural, some people have a hard time moving on with their life. Psychologists are able to assist patients in developing healthy coping mechanisms for the management of their feelings.

Most emos are people who have faced and dealt with trauma early on in their lives. They have seen the worst things in life, and they've been hurt, broken, and crippled by their pain. And this trauma controls much of their life because it goes by unresolved. It's a scar that keeps getting infected – an injury that only worsens with time.

This is why most emos look at life from the perspective of an outsider. They feel as though they are outcasts, even in their own skin, in their own homes, and with their friends. They feel as though they are strangers, even in a room full of people they know. This is just their trauma talking and bruising their damaged souls.

So what happens next?

Emos just walk on this fine glass, suffering each day – waiting until the day it finally breaks them and claims their life.

Solution

Trauma often results in shock, confusion, or depression. Sometimes, it's a mix of all three. Either way, it can be tough to deal with it. So, how do you deal with it? What's the solution to all this pain and misery? Here are a few things that you can do to relieve yourself of the pain:

1. Deal with trauma headfirst. Do not stay in denial. Don't overlook what's happening and what has happened. Face things instead of being in denial.

2. Find a support system. Find people that you can stick with – people you can be open and honest with. Talk through your pain with them. Be open and vulnerable; let them help you accept, acknowledge, and move past your pain.

3. Prioritize yourself and put yourself over all else. Self-care comes first, and it is essential for you to realize that, especially in your time of need.

4. Exercise and stay fit. It is said that studies help relieve stress. Movement helps your brain as it releases endorphins.

5. Seek professional help. Seeing a therapist can help with depression and coming to terms with trauma. Talking to a therapist helps with dealing with trauma and actually moving past it.

6. Jesus is always the answer to all your problems. Yes, life is hard. But God is able to cure any pain and damage in your life.

Conclusion

The frequency of bullying has steadily increased over the course of recent history. Sometimes, things work out in our favor, despite the fact that it is simpler to blame other people for being terrible and insensitive individuals. It is easy to get scarred by trauma, and in such a world, not only should we be understanding of other people and their plight. But we must also allow ourselves to heal. Moving on from trauma is never easy, but it is a crucial step that we must take for ourselves.

Poor Sleeping Habits

Problem

If you've been diagnosed with depression, it's possible that you have problems falling asleep or remaining asleep during the night. There is a rational explanation for that. There is a correlation between not getting enough sleep and feelings of depression. Insomnia, sometimes known as the inability to get asleep or remain asleep, is actually recognized as a typical symptom of depression. That is not to claim that depression is the only factor in cases of insomnia or other forms of disturbed sleep. It's worst for emos because they do have poor sleeping habits and usually suffer from insomnia. When you're unable to sleep properly, you end up getting hurt – physically and mentally. The scars of poor sleeping patterns run deeper than people expect. And this is why emos must work on repairing this 'damage.'

As an emo, it is possible that you face the following issues:

• You find it difficult to fall asleep, you have trouble staying asleep, and you wake up sooner than you would want (also known as insomnia)

• Have issues that prevent you from getting a good night's rest, such as anxiety attacks, traumatic flashbacks, nightmares, or psychosis.

• Sleep a lot – which may include sleeping at times when you want, or need, to be awake sleep a lot – which may include sleeping when you want, or need, to be awake when you find it difficult to wake up or get out of bed often feel tired or sleepy – this could be because you're not sleeping enough, not getting good quality sleep, due to mental or physical health issues.

Solution

Typical sleeping patterns are generally established during childhood. As we engage in these behaviors over an extended period of time, they eventually turn into habits. Insomnia is the inability to fall asleep or remain asleep during the night. You can often find relief from insomnia by adopting a few straightforward adjustments to your lifestyle. But, if you have maintained the same patterns of sleep for a number of years, it can take some time. Here are a few things that you can do to fix this:

• Keep a journal in which you record all of the things that are stressing you out. In this way, you can transfer your problems from your mind to paper, which will leave your thoughts more peaceful and make it easier for you to fall asleep.

• Increase your level of activity. Walk or engage in another form of exercise for at least half an hour on most days. Staying busy will exhaust you and force your brain to take a break which usually comes in the form of sleeping.

• Avoid taking naps during day time – try sleeping at nighttime only.

• If you are currently taking any medications, diet pills, herbs, or supplements, you should consult with your primary care physician on the potential affects these substances may have on your ability to sleep.

• Learn healthy strategies to deal with your stress.

• Acquaint yourself with various methods of unwinding, such as practicing yoga or meditation, listening to music, or engaging in guided visualization.

• Pay attention to the cues that your body sends you, such as when it wants you to slow down or take a break.

• Establish a regular pattern for your sleep and stick with this routine.

• Get into the habit of going to bed at roughly the same time every night, but no more than eight hours before the time you want to begin your day.

• You should steer clear of beverages that include caffeine or alcohol.

• It is recommended that you refrain from eating big meals at least two hours before your bedtime.

• Try your best to get up at the same hour every day if possible.

• Discover some hobbies that can help you wind down and relax before going to bed.

• Avoid screentime before bedtime.

• Be sure that your sleeping place is calm, dark, and at a temperature that is comfortable for you.

• You should limit doing anything that will raise your heart rate in the two hours leading up to going to bed.

• Seek professional help if you are experiencing feelings of sadness or depression.

Conclusion

Sleep is more important than we think, which is why it is necessary to have a proper sleep routine established. As an already stressed and emotional individual, you should avoid risking your health and further damaging your physical and mental health. Take care of yourself and stick to a healthy sleeping routine.

Poverty

Problem

We live in a materialistic world where economic disparity increases with every passing minute. In addition, the "show-off" lifestyle is becoming more prevalent due to the increase in connectivity, thanks to the internet. When people stop caring about others and start focusing on themselves, it leads to people caring less for each other and more for themselves.

Studies have proven that the percentage of suicides due to poverty is higher in teens than in any other age demographic. This is directly related to teens feeling like they'll never be as rich as the people they idolize over the internet or that they will never have equal opportunities in life. Hence, they decide to end things for themselves, under the notion that this will reduce the burden on their families and society.

Solution

The most basic way to combat this issue is to provide everyone with all the basic necessities. If charities become more efficient in using the donations provided to them. It can be done by ensuring that the money is utilized to set up camps rather than providing individuals with things they won't properly use. Giving them an opportunity to make a life for themselves will motivate them to strive harder. Setting up free camps for everyone to enroll themselves in would be a better way to tackle the poverty issue as a whole rather than for a small percentage that is struggling. Educational camps that teach specialization in a particular subject can allow one to acquire skills they can capitalize on. They can use these newly acquired skills to earn money.

It has been scientifically proven that staying busy (in an amount where you do not suffer from stress) can help tackle suicidal thoughts. In addition, it can also help one seek professional help to tackle suicidal tendencies. This can also help alleviate the issue of cyclical unemployment as training people will help increase the labor force and will eventually help the economy. This will provide a person with a purpose and help him feel like he's part of something bigger than himself.

Conclusion

Poverty is an issue that is often overlooked when issues contribute to the number of suicides in teens. This needs to be tackled using a simple rather than a complex solution with lower chances of working. There need to be awareness campaigns about how every individual contributes to society.

Another fairly simple way of tackling this issue would be for everyone to just have empathy for one another. Giving each other the benefit of the doubt as they don't know what the person is going through can help reduce some burden. The more fortunate can lend a hand to the less fortunate ones (financially). Scholarships and training camps can be provided to everyone to help tackle this issue.

Wrong People

Problem

Everyone needs friends. Not everyone is fortunate enough to befriend people easily. In addition, not everyone you befriend is a nice person. Some people have ulterior motives. People who struggle with making friends are usually people who have a chemical imbalance in their brains. They struggle to control and regulate their emotions sustainably. They often feel overwhelmed when they finally befriend someone, overlooking what their intentions are with them.

There are a lot of people that want to use other people to their advantage. Their intentions vary, ranging from using them for financial purposes to using them to feel better about themselves. In the latter's case, they usually make their friends the butt of every joke. They bully them under the guise of joking. They often use their secrets and insecurities against them, not realizing how it affects them. This is a common practice in the teenage demographic. When teens suffer in such conditions, they blame themselves for areas where they lack and eventually look for a way to escape their emotions- suicide.

Solution

Teens usually do not filter out what they say. It is an age where they only focus on themselves and their well-being. Even though that is a fair strategy to live by, they target others around them to help them feel better about themselves. In most cases, the closest and easiest target is their friends. They can be easily opened up to, as it is a vulnerable age. But this needs to change. Teens need to have each other's back. They need to reach out for help in simpler ways rather than manipulating others to gain something from them.

It is also necessary for teens to keep a check on what is being said about them in their friend circle. There needs to be independence in them. They should not feel like they will crumble if they do not have friends, nor should they feel like they will struggle to find new friends. Parents are also required to play a role in this. In the adolescent years, it is common for teens to push their parents away as their need for privacy grows. However, parts should still keep a check on their children so they can reach out if dark thoughts enter their minds when they start feeling like they aren't worthy of being alive.

Conclusion

A person's mindset transforms into what people around them think. This is why it is necessary for people, especially teens, to check what kind of friends they have. They should be surrounded by the positive energy that helps them grow. Teens must be surrounded by such energy, as these are the years that shape a person. If not kept in check, this will have an adverse effect. It can happen sooner or later. Sometimes, they might even feel like it is too late to find another way out. They need to feel supported at all times. So, if such a situation occurs, they are never afraid to cut the negative people off or to reach out for help.

Cyber Bullying

Problem

In a world where communication was made easier with the creation of the internet, it brought a new set of problems that needed to be tackled. The most major ease it brought was convenience. However, people stopped caring how words can affect someone, especially a stranger. People have started expressing their thoughts with no filter under the banner of "Freedom of Speech." However, this does more harm than good. People start attacking and bullying other people, dragging them through the dirt for what they do, believe in, and support. This is most often done by teenagers to other teenagers as they do not realize the value that their words hold. Those words can often have a lasting negative impact on a teenager's mind. What this leads to is depression and teenagers becoming way too conscious about a single aspect of theirs. They feel like they are not worthy just because a stranger on the internet doesn't deem them so. This leads to a high suicide rate among teenagers. The attacks are most often based on their skin color, body type, and social status.

Solution

Teenagers need to realize that words hold a lot of value. It brightens our day when a stranger compliments us. Likewise, it also ruins our day when a stranger passes a negative comment about us. Similarly, teenagers need to realize that destructive criticism about some can ruin their mood. When done in a capacity the victim cannot handle, it will lead to a negative mindset being formed in the victim's mind.

Everyone, including teenagers, should realize that cyberbullying is verbal abuse. And it is in no way acceptable. Attacking someone about an aspect of theirs is a crime. Just because there is zero accountability for the crime does not mean they can get away with it. Parents should strictly monitor what their child does on the internet, who he talks to, and what he says. In addition, social media companies should have filters in place to check what kind of messages are being exchanged.

Victims of this crime should realize that they are worthy of living. They are loved, supported, and cared for by someone in this world. It is not necessary for them to seek validation from strangers on the internet.

Conclusion

At the end of the day, the internet brings more benefits than it does harm. This does not mean that the cons should be ignored. Everyone on the internet should develop an accountability factor for themselves. They need to be mindful of what they say and who they say it to.

Moreover, people need to stop thinking that validation from a stranger is necessary for them. Everyone is beautiful in their own way. Being slim, white, and beautiful does not matter. Being a good person, however, does! Together, the issue of cyberbullying can be tackled and eradicated. All it needs is a little accountability and mindfulness.

Family Pressure

Problem

We live in a world where our worth is often measured by our success by society's standards. This often leads to guardians putting more pressure on their offspring's shoulders so that they can match the standards set by society and not be left behind. While every parent wants the best for their children, they often put too much pressure on their children's shoulders. Setting unrealistically high expectations from them and constant reminders and threats instills fear in them to match the expectations of their parents, no matter what. This leads to pressure often getting into the teenager's mind. This makes them live in constant fear of what will happen if they don't match the set expectations. They often feel like a failure and end up committing suicide out of fear that they will be deemed a failure.

Solution

It needs to be realized by all parents that standards set by society are not a reliable scale to measure their children's success. Everyone has a unique set of skills. Rather than telling their children what they should be, they should tell their kids to play to their strengths. Every parent knows their child, so it should not be too difficult to point out their strengths to them. In case they do not know, it is required by every parent to help them discover their strengths.

It needs to be realized by every teenager that the standards set by society are toxic and unreliable. The fear of failing in the eyes of society is a fear that they should not take seriously. Instead, they should set goals and standards for themselves and plan out their journey according to them. They should not let words get the best of them, and they need to realize that it is okay to be a little behind everyone else.

Conclusion

Words carry a lot of weight. Guardians need to realize that instead of pushing them to match society's standards, they should push them to be the best version of themselves. Personal growth is more important than growth that society deems necessary. In addition, it is okay to be a bit slow. Everyone does not have the same rate of growth as everyone else.

Teenagers need to realize that they are worth more than the goals that have been set for them by society. Running after goals that don't matter to them personally will only result in them losing a part of themselves that they cherished. They need to set goals for themselves that allow them to grow as a person.

Psychological Disorder

Problem

It is more prevalent than one might imagine for adolescents to struggle with mental health issues. Teens who are raised in environments where they are not given adequate attention and care are more likely to develop psychiatric illnesses, which are a contributing factor to the high number of teen suicides that occur around the world. It is possible for a teen to develop mental illnesses as a result of insufficient care, neglect, or abuse. This can leave a teen with the idea that they don't belong in this world and that everyone else would be better off without them being there. They feel like a burden and often seek for a way out. Research has shown that 85 to 95% of people who die by suicide have a diagnosable mental health condition at the time of their death. This is a fact that everyone should think about.

Solution

The quality of a child's relationship with his or her parents is a critical factor in determining whether or not the teenager will go on to develop psychological problems. If young people are brought up to believe that they are deserving of love and care, then they are more likely to believe that they have a purpose in life and work toward achieving that purpose. When their child is going through a difficult moment, most of the time, it is very easy for parents to recognize it. As soon as this is detected, prompt action needs to be taken in response to it. They ought to look into any and all potential remedies, including treatment for their child, in an effort to solve the problem that their child is having.

Teenagers should not be reluctant to ask for assistance out of fear. A constructive discussion about the problems they are facing has the potential to bring about an enormous amount of progress in improving their position. They need to hash out their difficulties through conversation. They need to be made aware of the crisis hotlines that are available to them so that they can seek and get assistance.

Conclusion

One might be led to believe that psychological disorders are responsible for a much lower percentage of teen suicides than is actually the case, despite the fact that this is a widely held misconception. As a result, this is a problem that ought not to be taken lightly at all. Anyone who has the ability to provide supervision, including parents, teachers, guardians, older siblings, and anyone else, should be aware of the symptoms that can be used to diagnose a psychological disorder. They need to be well-versed in how to deal with these issues when they are brought to their attention, and they need to move quickly to take action before it is too late.

Developmental Delays

Problem

Not every teen develops at the same rate. The development of the body is an area where a lot of scientific research has taken place. But the more research is conducted, the more questions arise from it. Science has proven that the front lobe of the brain does not fully develop until the age of 25. Teens running around with an underdeveloped brain is a recipe for disaster. So, teens that have stunned or slow growth are often the target of bullies that don't fully understand the weight of the words they are spewing. This leads to teens often believing that they are different than others. Consequently, they feel alienated and look for a solution to end their problem. More often than not, suicide is the answer that they find for themselves. They turn to this option as they believe this is their only way out. Their brain has not formed properly; therefore, they do not make the right decisions, unfortunately.

Solution

In order to tackle this issue, awareness must be spread. There is also self-accountability involved on everyone's part. Teens need to realize that it is normal to grow at a different rate than others around them. The rate of their growth does not define them. They should be taught that they are worthy of being alive. However, others around the aforementioned teens should be careful of what they tell the teens. Words have a lot of weight; hence they should not be taken lightly. They should not be based if they're different from others. Rather it should be normalized to be different from others. They should be taught that it is okay to be a bit behind everyone else in their company. Parents and guardians also need to step in to play their part. Every parent knows the flaws and shortcomings of their child. They should not use harsh words when punishing or scolding them, as certain words can trigger these dark thoughts when they are directed toward their insecurities.

Conclusion

Growth is relative. Not everyone grows at the same rate. This is a fact most people ignore. In addition, this is an issue that can be nipped in the bud if small steps are taken. However, this is also an issue where everyone involved plays a vital role in the elimination of this issue. People should comfort others that are going through a tough time due to this issue. Appearance, body type, and intellectual capacity are a few examples of things that can be slow during the developmental stages of a teen. These problems and others like these should not be made of.

Sexual Abuse

Problem

In many cases, teens are exploited for sex. This is a federal crime, but as teenagers, this fact is unknown to them. People around them use their naivety, vulnerability, and lack of resources to their advantage. They are often offered easy access to their needs if exchange for sexual favors. They readily agree or are forced to agree to it under pressure. The reality of the situation hits them later in their life. By that time, they often decide it is too late to take legal action against them. Moreover, they fail to see a point in pursuing a legal course of action against their wrongdoings to hold them accountable. People do not think about the repercussion of asking for such favors. These people are used to living with a guilty conscious and do not think about what they're doing.

Solution

Teenagers should receive sex education. The most logical way to do this would be to introduce a course in their curriculum. This way, they can get an education about what sex is, who they should have it with, and when is the right time to have it. Furthermore, they will know what to do if you're being forced or coerced into a position to have sex with someone you do not consent to have sex with. They should be taught that no such behavior is to be tolerated and that they need to raise their voice against it. They should also be taught self-defense strategies that can help teenagers escape from such situations.

Conclusion

It is a crime to seek sexual favors from teenagers. Teenagers should be made aware that it is wrong on every level. Abuse of a victim's sexuality can be a significant contributor to the act of suicide by a teen. Abuse victims may suffer from feelings of shame, guilt, and helplessness, all of which can contribute to the development of depression and a loss of hope. This can lead to thoughts and actions of self-harm or suicide.

Education is the most effective tool for protecting young people from being sexually abused. Teenagers should have their parents, teachers, and other adults who care for them educate them about the dangers of sexual abuse and teach them how to identify abusive behavior. It is also important to provide a safe and supportive environment for teenagers so that they will feel comfortable reporting any instances of abuse that they may have witnessed.

Teenagers who have been victims of sexual abuse may benefit from talking to a counselor and participating in therapy. They can assist victims in working through the feelings that they are experiencing and in developing coping mechanisms. In addition, the authorities should take severe action against people who sexually abuse children in order to send a clear message that this kind of behavior will not be tolerated.

Ease of Access to Firearms

Problem

One of the most common ways for young people to take their own lives is by shooting themselves. People have a propensity to frequently overlook this extremely important aspect. There is a common misconception that obtaining firearms is significantly more difficult than it actually is. It is not difficult for a young person who is desperate and determined to find a way out to obtain firearms. In the majority of cases, adolescents gain access to firearms and ammunition by engaging in illegal trades or by stealing the weapon of another individual. Teenagers who feel they have reached their breaking point and must find a way out often turn to this method because they believe it is a simpler and less distressing way to end their lives than other options. Sadly, that does not appear to be the case. Unfortunately, that is not the case. Botched efforts are more common than one might believe.

Solution

Reduced use of firearms is the most important step that needs to be taken in order to regain control of the situation. This is the most important action that needs to be taken. It is unacceptable to allow individuals to own or sell firearms. This would result in a reduction in the number of people who take their own lives using firearms. It should be possible for people who already possess them to return them in exchange for monetary compensation if this proposal is approved. In addition, people who still own guns should be required to undergo psychiatric evaluations so that it can be determined whether or not they are fit enough to be in possession of such a potent weapon. In addition, owners ought to store their firearms out of sight and away from other members of the household who are not fully aware of the potential danger posed by a firearm.

There is a misconception that has been projected on teenagers through movies and TV shows: Suicide through the use of guns leads to a painless and quick death. That is not true. Death through the use of a gun is painful and slow. More often than not, a wrong aim can lead to damage being inflicted on the body that is not reversible. This leads to even more agony for the victim.

Conclusion

The availability of firearms is a risk for society. Teenagers are the most susceptible age group, and as a result, they are the ones who fall victim to this horrible invention. They do not have a complete comprehension of the power that it possesses. As a result, they have an inaccurate perception of it and don't give it the consideration it deserves before employing it. Control should be maintained over the distribution, and a minimum number of people should be considered owners. If nothing is done to stop it, this danger will only get worse over time. Therefore, it is necessary for governments to take action on this issue and find a viable course of action to eradicate and minimize this threat that is currently being faced before the life of another innocent teen is lost.

Sexual Orientation

Problem

We live in a past paced world where more advancements are made every day. We progress in every aspect and gain more freedom and independence. However, everyone does not let others feel comfortable. Teenagers are often targeted or abused in regard to their gender and sexual orientation. People feel like they are entitled to an opinion on what they should be and feel like. So, they often tell teenagers who do not feel comfortable in their own bodies how they should feel about themselves. They fail to realize what the teenager feels like in their body. People often hurl hurtful comments towards teenagers, making an effort to express themselves how they feel. This leads to teenagers feeling like they are outcasts and they do not deserve a place in society. This leads to dark thoughts manifesting in a teenager's mind. They look for a way out, which in most cases is suicide.

Solution

People should realize that it is okay for others to express themselves as they deem necessary. They should broaden their understanding of what norms have led them to believe. We live in a world where it is allowed to freely express one's self. So, they should be more accepting of teenagers who are opening up to them and expressing themselves. It is crucial that they come to the realization that it takes a lot of confidence on the teenager's part to accept themselves for what they are and then to present to the world how they feel comfortable. They should not make anyone feel like someone they aren't, that too in their own body. Teenagers need to realize that it is okay to be whatever they are. It is a natural feeling, and they shouldn't feel like they need to be anything other than what they are to please the world.

Conclusion

People are wrong to pressure teenagers into imagining they are something other than who they really are. It runs counter to the very ideals upon which modern society is constructed. Teenagers need to be treated with respect and taught to respect others. The world is evolving, and there are many open-minded people in it. Teens should know that they can choose to ignore the opinions of those who cannot accept them for who they are. It's important to avoid absorbing anyone else's negativity. Young people should make it clear to those who radiate negativity that they will not tolerate it.

Family History

Problem

Science has proven that teenagers who have parents that committed suicide are two and a half times more likely to commit suicide themselves compared with those without a similar family history. Parents might have committed suicide due to unrelated reasons, but their parting from their offspring is sure to leave a lasting impact on them. Hence, these thoughts can turn really dark really quickly. In most cases, parents commit suicide due to a medical condition. This should be taken into consideration as there is a high possibility that their offspring might be suffering from a similar condition as the parents. In many cases, early signs are ignored, and the correct course of action is not taken. Therefore, it leads to a sad end for the victim when it all could have been easily avoided if the correct steps to combat the issue had been taken.

Solution

A solution for these problems requires it to be a multi-faceted approach. Firstly, psychiatric evaluations should be taken by family members of those who have gone through the struggle of losing a loved one to suicide. This can help doctors determine of other family members are healthy enough to combat the issue. Secondly, behavior changes should be noticed by all family members. Close attention should be paid to all family members behavior, and everyone in the family should be encouraged to talk about what they feel like and share what they have to say. Medical examinations and DNA tests should be taken to see if one is at risk of developing a mental issue.

Conclusion

Humans are social beings. They interact with others with similar interests and grow as a person. Likewise, traits are inherited and can be passed down from generation to generation. It is necessary for parents to find their medical history and check their offspring's medical history as well. As soon as a symptom is detected, swift action should be taken to correct it. This is a problem that should be nipped in the bud. With medical advancements taking place in every passing second and new DNA tests being made available to the public, it is now easier than ever to seek medical attention. Therefore, all crucial steps to prevent this should be taken as soon as possible.

Loss and Grief

Problem

Part of being human means that you will have to experience loss and grief during your lifetime. However, experiencing said emotions can leave a lasting impact on one's social and emotional well-being. Often, people, including teenagers, experience a drastic amount of trauma. If this trauma is not processed in a healthy manner, it can lead to a lot of problems. People who fail to process their emotions in a suitable manner can often develop issues such as physical health issues, mental health disorders, emotional distress, and changes in behavior. Often, teenagers who are at this age do not have a brain that has finished developing. When they go through the loss of a loved one and do not find an outlet to express how they feel or feel like they cannot function without the person they have lost, dark thoughts often start developing in their mind. In most cases, they believe decide that they cannot function without the presence of their loved one. So, they decide to commit suicide in order to join them.

Solution

It is important for teenagers and all people who experience loss and grief to realize that everyone has to die one day. That is an essential part of a person's life. Their end may come at a time that no one is expecting. This is why teenagers should develop an understanding that life eventually does come to an end. But that does not mean that the teenager should believe that there is no purpose for them after their loved one is taken away from them. They need to understand that they serve a different purpose from their loved ones and are independent. It is the parents' and guardians' responsibility to teach their children about how a life cycle works. Furthermore, parents and guardians should tell their children how to process emotions in a healthy and suitable manner. Parents should act as an outlet for their offspring to express their emotions. In their child does not feel like their parents are the right outlet, then parents should allow them to contact a therapist to seek help. Communication is a simple solution that can help prevent such a problem. It is important to seek help at the beginning of such a phase. This is a problem that can be fatal if not dealt with swiftly as soon as it manifests.

Conclusion

The emotion of loss and grief are such that they can manifest into bigger issues if they are overlooked. It can lead to mental and physical issues. Issues such as breathing problems, panic attacks, depression, and feeling physically weak can occur. It is important for parents, guardians, and people who accompany those who are grieving to keep an eye out to notice signs. They should converse with victims of such situations, helping them feel like they are not alone and that they can process emotions with the passage of time. This is an issue that can be solved by utilizing simple techniques.

Environmental Factors

Problem

When attempting to identify the causes of suicide, it is common to leave out environmental factors. Since few people consider it a possible cause, it is frequently overlooked. However, a lot of suicides have to do with the conditions that people are living in. Living in a high-stress or high-crime area is one example of such a circumstance. These may elevate the possibility of suicidal thinking and actions. The effects of working and living in such a place can be detrimental. The mental toll of persistent anxiety builds up over time. Teenagers are particularly vulnerable because they have not yet developed effective coping mechanisms. The pressure and stress of their predicament cause them to form negative perceptions of themselves. This typically takes the form of suicidal ideation and culminates in the adolescent child putting those ideas into action by taking their own life.

Solution

To combat this issue, a community-based strategy must be implemented. This is a problem that must be addressed at its core. The most essential aspect of this strategy must be fostering social support. It is necessary to establish strong support networks where these issues can be addressed; they can help individuals feel connected and provide a sense of belonging and purpose. This can drastically reduce the risk of suicide among adolescents, who are the most susceptible. As vulnerable individuals, they are the ones who fail to find a solution to their problems the majority of the time.

Additionally, the issues must be addressed, and awareness must be spread. Community safety should be prioritized, and community safety programs must be implemented. It is necessary to establish emergency response programs and task forces in order to mitigate the aforementioned environmental factors.

Conclusion

Environmental factors can sometimes prove to be a much bigger problem than one might initially think. Living in an environment that is high in stress and pressure on a day-to-day basis can add up to a point where it may be tempting for a young person to give in to the suicidal ideas that are forming in their head. Because of the way it was designed, the human brain requires leisure time in order to function properly. If an individual is placed in a situation where they are expected to live and function in a high-stress environment on a consistent basis, suicidal thoughts will begin to form in their mind, and they will eventually act on those thoughts. To find a solution to this problem, the community as a whole needs to get involved. People need to work together to support one another and make an effort to ensure that everyone feels secure and at ease.

Cultural factors

Problem

Teenagers in this generation are given freedom without supervision and guidance. This leads to an adolescent child with an underdeveloped brain feeling like they are the best judge of their situation. They believe they do not need to take anyone's advice on the decisions they make. Without supervision, they are exposed to social media, movies, and television, where suicide culture is being normalized. They do not realize that movies are not real and are produced for consumption as a means of entertainment. Among teenagers, it is deemed cool to be independent and not to seek help. It is normal for teenagers to demand privacy, so it becomes difficult for parents and guardians to keep an eye out and supervise their activities. When dark thoughts start forming in teenagers' minds, they are too scared to reach out for help and often end up committing suicide.

Solution

The government needs to take an active role in controlling the types of media that are made available to the general public in order to effectively address this problem. They ought to keep in mind that children of varying ages consume said media, and they ought to exercise control over the kind of message that is communicated to the children. It should be made clear that consuming media, even when there are warnings that are put in place to deter teenagers or children from consuming it, is not cool. Parents need to force themselves into their children's lives and examine what sort of media is being consumed by them. Parental supervision programs should be launched by all companies to reduce the amount of screen time children under the age of 18 consume. Furthermore, these programs should also be able to allow parents to see what sort of media is being consumed by their young ones. It should be made clear that reaching out is not something to be ashamed of.

Conclusion

The role of media in the rate of suicides among teenagers is frequently not paid enough attention to. If suicide culture is normalized and movies deliver the message that it is a viable solution to one's problems, teenagers will be led to believe that it is okay for them to act out their dark thoughts. Instead of reaching out because they feel it is not cool, they end up committing suicide, only out of the fear of being deemed uncool if they reach out for help. There should be strict control on what mass media is delivered to the public for consumption. The subliminal and contextual meaning of such media should be kept in check. Failure to do so will allow teenagers to act out on their dark thoughts. Moreover, addressing the cultural stigma surrounding mental health can encourage individuals to seek help when they need it, reducing the risk of suicide.

Military Service or Combat Exposure

Problem

Often, teenagers who consider themselves academic failures start to believe they cannot survive in the real world. They are led to believe they will struggle to find jobs and a steady source of income. Therefore, they will be left alone, homeless, and struggling. It is a frequent practice among such teenagers who face such a situation to look for a foolproof, easy-to-follow plan that can guarantee a steady source of income. So, they enroll to join the army in the hopes that they can retire after doing a few tours, and since you can get a pension with benefits that start the day you leave, they believe it is an easy way to get a regular salary as early as age 37. What becomes a problem is that these teenagers have not yet experienced the real world and are provided with combat exposure that can scar their underdeveloped brains for life. What becomes another layer of this issue is the fact that these teenagers believe that military service and combat exposure are the same as the ones they are subjected to in the video games that they play. It is often too late before they realize how messed up being a part of the military is.

Solution

The problem lies in the hiring of recruits. Recruiters look for individuals suited physically for the job and often overlook the mental aspect required for the job. While it is true that military service can help secure a steady stream of income, it requires teenagers to lose a part of themselves that they are too young to lose. Teenagers often want to prove their worth and act tough. Hence, they sign up without thinking it through, believing how hard it could be to serve a few years in the military.

The atrocities that they are subjected to while on tours are horrifying situations that no teenager should have to experience. If they do not get affected while they're on active service, they suffer from mental illnesses, most often in the form of PTSD, when they return back home. Signs of PTSD from serving in the military include:

• Temper tantrums and other displays of fury.

• Extreme nervousness and anxiety.

• Stress and exhaustion.

• Apathy and depression.

• Appetite loss.

• Sleep disturbances.

• Alterations in conduct or character.

When teenagers return from duty, they are often too scared to talk about the atrocities that they have seen as the military has made them adopt the "strong-independent" persona. On numerous occasions, they cannot bring themselves to talk to seek professional help and go to a therapist, succumbing to their dark thoughts and committing suicide.

Conclusion

Teenagers are not built to serve in the military. Their young brains are still under development, and they are naïve. In their naivety, they agree to serve a few years in the military, believing that it is a good way to contribute to society. Teenagers are too young to make such big decisions on their own. Recruiters often promise them that they'll be alright and their fellow comrades will look out for them. While they can look out for on duty, they cannot be there all the time. In addition, serving in the military requires a person to adopt a "though-guy" persona. So, they are afraid to reach out to someone when they need help. In conclusion, there should be apprehensive psychological tests that should be taken when enrolling a teenager to ensure they will not suffer from a mental illness upon returning. Furthermore, it should be mandated for them to have therapy sessions on a regular basis to further eliminate the risk of developing such an illness.

Postpartum depression or anxiety

Problem

Teenage pregnancy is common. At an age where a person's mind has not finished fully developing, it is unreasonable for them to take on such a huge responsibility. However, it is a frequent occurrence that teenagers go through the process of becoming a parent. They believe that they are old enough to raise and take care of a child. Another reason for the rise in the number of teenage pregnancies is the lack of awareness and use of contraceptives among teenagers. Teenagers often start partaking in sexual activities at an age when they are experiencing puberty. They are not fully aware of how the human body works. Hence, teenage pregnancies can occur at stages of life where the pregnant individual's brain and body have not fully finished developing. This leads to complications in pregnancy which include the likes of premature birth, delivering a stillborn baby, and systemic infections. The loss of a child at such a stage in life leads to depression and anxiety. With an underdeveloped brain reeling from such a great loss of life, parents are often led to fend for themselves. This results in them developing anxiety and depression. Not wanting to trouble their spouses, they seek a way out, usually in the shape of suicide. Young parents often fail to see that suicide is a serious and irreversible act that can have devastating consequences for the individual and their loved ones.

Solution

Awareness is the best solution to the problem of teenage pregnancies. Parents of teenagers need to take it upon themselves to let their offspring know that it is okay to explore their sexuality, but also guide them on how they need to protect themselves and their partner. Proper sex-ed should be provided by the parents to their teenagers, which should make them aware of the need for the use of contraceptives. In addition, they should guide them on how to acquire protection and how to protect themselves and avoid the transmission of sexual diseases. Well-formed courses on sexual education should be provided in school. Parents who experience pregnancy in their teenage tears should be supported and consult a doctor who can guide them on what the best path is for them to take to minimize the risk for the unborn child and the mother. Furthermore, couples therapy can be an additional way to reduce the risk of developing a mental illness in case of a failed delivery of the child. It can help strengthen the relationship of the parents and help them be guided on what the best path is for them moving forward, reeling from such a huge loss.

Conclusion

It is important for teenagers to realize that pregnancy is a huge step that they should be certain that it is a step that they want to take. Teenagers have brains and bodies that are in the process of being developed. Hence, they are not the best judge of their situation. Since their body has not fully gone through the developmental stage, they are not ready to carry life in said body. Mothers are often unaware of such facts, believing that since they are female, they can carry life at any stage of their life. So, it is necessary for parents and guardians to provide them with information about how they can go safely through the process of exploring their bodies and minimize the risk of transmission of an STD or, worse, pregnancy. Contraceptives should be made readily available for teenagers, and proper sexual education should be provided to such individuals.

Eating Disorders or Body Dysmorphia

Problem

In the teenage years of life, a person, their body goes through the process of puberty. In this process, the body goes through developmental changes. People go through a lot of changes. They experience changes mentally and physically. As a person is growing up, they experience a change in appetite as well. Coupled with the experiences one has as a teenager, it is a frequent occurrence for them to develop eating disorders. Eating disorders can lead to body dysmorphia. Body dysmorphia is a common and severe disorder, yet it is underrecognized and underdiagnosed. In BDD, a person starts believing that they have an ugly body. It is important to note that these disorders are prevalent among teenagers. Men and females are affected by it in an equal ratio. What makes the problem worse is the fact that bullying culture makes a victim of such a disorder feel insecure about themselves. As their body is going through development, teenagers can do only so much to change their body until it develops completely. So, they look for a way out - Suicide.

Solution

It is necessary for teenagers to realize that what they're going through is a natural process. In it, it is normal for your body type to change. The change in appetite is part of a natural reaction that the body generates as it needs more food in order to grow. However, they do not feel ashamed of their body. If they feel that their diet is not healthy or unnatural, they should seek professional advice from a dietician. Parents should support their young ones who are a victim of body dysmorphia. Furthermore, they should keep an eye out for the food that their teen eats. In addition, keeping a channel of communication open with them can help them talk about how they feel and what they're going through. Therapy can be an option to help discuss how a teenager feels about their body. Eating disorders can be solved using the solutions listed below:

• Ask your doctor or therapist for a referral.

• Call local hospitals and universities.

• Call local eating disorder centers and clinics.

• Visit your school's counseling center.

• Call a helpline

Furthermore, it is important for every teenager to be accepted just the way they are and to let them know that they are more than just their body. The following tips can help a teenager feel better about their body:

• Listen to your feelings.

• Listen to your body.

• Accept yourself.

• Love yourself.

Conclusion

This is a disorder that is most prevalent in teenagers. Hence, it deserves special attention in order to minimize the number of suicides that take place due to this issue. Eating disorders are fairly easy to develop as a person can often overlook the amount of calories being consumed. Hence, their parents should step in to guide them about the dangers associated with eating disorders. BDD is linked with eating disorders, as teenagers who suffer from an eating disorder often fall prey to BDD. Once a teenager falls victim to BDD, it becomes really difficult for them to see themselves in a different light, one that makes them feel better about themselves. Teenagers should be taught about what a healthy calorie intake looks like, and schools should have a dietician made available. Therapists need to raise awareness of the issue as well.

Medication Side Effects

Overview

Babies being born or being diagnosed with a disease or a disorder is a fairly common occurrence. Hence, it forces them to be on medication through the developmental stage of their life. Often, the doctors that diagnosed them fail to reveal to the parents that the medication prescribed to them has side effects. In most cases, there are physical side effects. But a considerable percentage of such cases with such children leave mental side effects. Chemical imbalance in the brain during the developmental stage of life can be detrimental to health. Thoughts and ideas are not formed correctly in the brain and cloud the judgment of the individual that has suffered through such a condition at such an early age. Pediatricians and junior doctors who might have prescribed them do not reveal the side effects of the medication they prescribe to such individuals. Parents, unaware of the suffering their child has to bear, take no action whatsoever to prevent their child from acting on any dark thoughts that might be forming in their brain. It is often too late by the time their parents or guardians might realize what their child has suffered through.

Solution

It is the parent's duty to supervise their children's activities. They need to perform their duty and keep a channel of communication open if they are aware of the fact that their young one is on prescribed medication. It is their part to research the potential side effects of the drugs that are being consumed by their young child on a daily basis. They should seek professional help from doctors and therapists besides the one who has been employed by them to take off their child. Children need to talk to their parents and ask for help when dark thoughts start forming in their brains. There are symptoms that can help determine what kind of mood your child is in. The following symptoms indicate that your child is going through a tough time.

• Social withdrawal

• Appetite changes

• Sleep disturbances

• Mood swings

• Changes in behavior

Parents should keep an eye out for the following symptoms if their offspring have been on medication for a considerable amount of time.

Conclusion

Chemical imbalance in the brain is not a problem that should be overlooked, especially if the individual in question is a teenager. It is easy to believe what people are saying when your judgment is clouded. Left alone with no one to seek help from, teenagers often look to act out their dark thoughts. Parents should read their child's body language and act swiftly before their teenager acts in a way their actions cannot be reversed. Parents should know that if their child refuses to keep, becomes socially reclusive, or if their child refuses to talk to anyone about how they are progressing in life, something is wrong. They should know that their child does not feel okay and that they should intervene before they lose their child forever.

Fear of Punishment or Legal Consequences

Overview

Children are naïve. They make mistakes and learn from them. Oftentimes, parents adopt a strict parenting approach and tell their kids that they are not allowed to mess up, or they will face harsh consequences. While it is not fair to instill such fear into the hearts of such young and innocent beings, parents go ahead and punish their kids harshly when they do something against their orders. Stealing. Lying and damaging someone else's property are examples of such actions that usually get teenagers in trouble with their strict parents. When they inevitably mess up, they cannot rely on their parents to get them out of trouble. Threatened with legal consequences and the fear of punishment, they end up committing suicide, believing that there is no way out for them. Parents should play their role to protect their children and teach them lessons softly and in a way that they receive them efficiently.

Solution

Parents should play their role as they were meant to. Instead of scaring them with punishment, they should choose to explain to their children why doing a certain action is not something they advise. They should relay their message in a soft manner. Teenagers might believe they are tough and can handle any situation, but they are not above the law. Parents should guide their children about the basics of law. Furthermore, parents should ensure their teens that they are there for them in any situation. Teenagers should refrain from committing such actions that are illegal. It is normal for teenagers to be curious, but they should not let curiosity get the best of them. Parents should tell their young ones that there is always a better solution to their problems than committing suicide. Parents should always be available to solve their teenager's problems and never leave them on their own to deal with their problems on their own.

Conclusion

While no one is above the law, suicide is not the solution. This is the message that parents should be teaching their adolescent children. Harsh punishments and scolding children are not acceptable ways of teaching children what is right and what is wrong. Children are young and curious. It is natural for curiosity to get the best of them and for them to make the wrong decisions in life. Rather than punishing them for their actions, it is better for them to explain to them softly why what they did is wrong. This ensures that a child learns from their experience and never repeats their mistake. Additionally, if they do mess up, parents should always be available to get them out of trouble. Lastly, teenagers should realize that suicide is not the solution. No matter how difficult a situation might look, there is always a way out.

Exposure to Toxic or Stressful Work Environments

Overview

To start working at an early age is a normal practice. Most people start working at 14-15 years of age. At this age, their body might be ready to work long hours and take on the physical strain that comes with working a job. However, it is not an age where their brain can make decisions where it can decide what is better for themselves. At this age, children believe having a steady stream of income is more important than being physically healthy. This is all due to a lack of development in their brain at such an age. It is a barbaric practice for children to work jobs that healthy adults struggle to work. Workplaces can often be toxic and, generally, an unhealthy place to spend long hours in. Instead of helping a teenager grow, it stuns their growth and changes their mindset. This, in turn, coupled with the stress of maintaining their employment status, teenagers often are afraid to reach out or quit. This leads to them thinking that they will never be equal to their peers, and dark thoughts start developing in their brains. Consequently, this leads to them committing suicide at an early age, all due to the stress of working.

Solution

Employers should prioritize the psychological well-being of their employees, including younger workers. Implementing psychological evaluation tests during the hiring process can assess an individual's mental readiness for a role, reducing the risk of placing undue stress on them. Providing suitable roles aligned with their abilities and experience is crucial. Teenagers may have limited skills and emotional maturity, so assigning tasks within their capabilities creates a supportive work environment.

Parents play a vital role in supporting their working children. Regular conversations help assess their adjustment and workload. Parents should ensure their child isn't overworked or exploited. Open communication encourages children to express concerns. Parents should be aware of their child's rights, educating them on fair labor practices such as minimum wage and workplace safety. By staying involved and supportive, parents can advocate for their child's well-being.

By prioritizing psychological evaluation, suitable roles, and open communication, employers and parents contribute to a positive work experience for young workers. This approach promotes their growth, skill development, and confidence. Creating a supportive work environment helps teenagers thrive and fosters a healthy work-life balance. It also instills the importance of employee well-being, benefiting workers of all ages. Employers and parents working together ensure a positive work experience and lay the groundwork for young workers' future success.

Conclusion

While the 'I started working at an early age lifestyle is now normalized and encouraged, it should be realized that this was only introduced as inflation grew and people's ability to live a comfortable quality of life diminished. Teenagers do not have the ability to work long hours and manage a lifestyle that they should have at such an age. Hence, sooner or later, it comes to haunt them. They are either tortured and exploited by their peers who keep piling work on them or have them work very long hours. Contrary to popular belief, most teenagers who work are underpaid and overworked. Because of their young age, they fail to voice their concerns. And due to the fear of losing their job, they never get around to voicing their concerns. When dark thoughts start forming in their brains, they are left to fend for themselves, believing they are alone in fighting this battle. They often end up committing suicide. By taking sympathy and empathy and giving young employees the benefit of the doubt, this dark conclusion to their life can be easily avoided.

Exposure to Violence or Trauma in the Media

Overview

The impact of media violence on individuals' brains is a highly debated topic. While disclaimers and content warnings are often used to address concerns, the push for more realistic content blurs the boundary between reality and fiction. As advancements in technology enable the creation of visually stunning and lifelike portrayals of violence, viewers can easily forget that they are observing staged performances. This psychological immersion raises significant questions about the potential consequences. Moreover, there is a growing concern about the presence of subliminal messages within movies and video games. Advertisers have long used subliminal techniques to influence consumer behavior, and it is not far-fetched to imagine that media creators might employ similar strategies. Particularly vulnerable demographics, such as teenagers who are still developing their own sense of right and wrong, may be more susceptible to these messages. This vulnerability, coupled with the blurring of real and fake, can lead to confusion and an acceptance of dark thoughts that would otherwise be dismissed. Navigating the delicate balance between artistic expression, consumer demand, and responsible content creation is crucial. It is essential for society to promote critical thinking skills that enable individuals to discern between entertainment and real-life consequences. This emphasis on critical thinking becomes even more crucial for teenagers as they grapple with the challenges of self-identity and moral development. By fostering an environment that encourages thoughtful analysis, we can mitigate potential negative effects and help individuals make informed choices about the media they consume.

Solution

The simplest solution to address the impact of media violence on individuals, particularly teenagers, would involve a combined effort from studios, parents, and open conversations. Studios should take responsibility by clearly placing age guidance warnings and providing detailed descriptions of their content. This helps parents make informed decisions about what their children can safely consume, reducing the chances of them adopting misguided ideas from the media. Mandating studios to include warnings not only about explicit violence but also about any potential subliminal messages is crucial. By making viewers aware of hidden or subtle influences, individuals can approach the content with a more discerning mindset. This transparency empowers both parents and viewers to make conscious choices based on their values and protect against any potential negative effects.

In addition to the role of studios, parents must play an active role in their children's media consumption. By taking an interest in the content their children engage with and actively monitoring their activities, parents can create a safer environment. Open conversations about the media being consumed, and discussing the themes, messages, and values depicted are essential. This allows parents to provide guidance, address any misconceptions, and reinforce appropriate behavior, ultimately helping teenagers navigate the distinction between fiction and reality. Furthermore, establishing clear boundaries and rules around media consumption can contribute to a healthier viewing experience. Setting screen time limits, implementing parental controls, and engaging in shared activities that promote alternative forms of entertainment and learning can offer a balanced approach.

By combining the efforts of studios, responsible parenting, open dialogue, and thoughtful monitoring, we can mitigate the potential negative impact of media violence on individuals. This approach ensures that individuals, especially teenagers, are exposed to content that aligns with their developmental needs and promotes responsible behavior.

Conclusion

This is an important issue that is often overlooked. Parents don't want to fulfill their duties as they are meant to, and studios just want as much money as they can. However, there is accountability that needs to be taken on both ends. Studios need to realize the power they hold and decide to use it in a responsible, more socially acceptable manner. Parents, on the other hand, cannot solely rely on studios to play their parts. They should be ready to step in and help guide their young ones. Being open to talking about what the media is portraying can be a helpful way of avoiding a dark fate.

Stigma Around Mental Health

Overview

Discussing mental health can be challenging due to the persisting negative connotations and misconceptions surrounding the topic. Unfortunately, society often stigmatizes individuals facing mental health struggles, labeling them as weaker or less valuable members of the community. The pervasive lack of understanding leads people to underestimate the profound impact their words can have on those experiencing such unfortunate circumstances. It is essential for society to recognize that mental health issues can affect anyone, irrespective of their physical strength or outward appearance. Rather than subjecting individuals to ridicule or judgment, we should prioritize providing them with the support and understanding they need during their difficult journey. Mental health challenges can be debilitating, and it takes immense strength and courage for someone to confront and address their inner struggles. Offering empathy, compassion, and non-judgmental support can make a world of difference to those battling mental health issues. The negative connotations attached to mental health discussions perpetuate stigma and hinder progress. It is essential for society to shift its perspective, understanding that mental health struggles can affect anyone and should not be met with ridicule or judgment.

Solution

Addressing the issue of mental health stigma requires a collective effort and a willingness to learn and educate ourselves. Individuals must take it upon themselves to actively seek knowledge and understanding about how mental health is affected, as well as the challenges faced by those experiencing it. By educating ourselves, we can break down the barriers of ignorance and misconception. When we become acquainted with someone going through a tough time, it is crucial to extend our support and love to them. Making them feel heard, valued, and understood can have a profound impact on their well-being. Simply reminding them that they are not alone in their struggles can provide comfort and solace. It is essential to foster an environment where individuals feel safe to openly express their emotions and seek help without fear of judgment or rejection. Overcoming mental health stigma requires a united front from society. It is through our combined efforts that we can challenge and change the negative connotations attached to mental health. By engaging in open conversations, sharing personal experiences, and advocating for mental health awareness, we can break down the barriers and create a culture of acceptance and support.

Conclusion

In a healthy and inclusive society, it is vital for every individual to recognize and acknowledge their inherent value and worth. This applies equally to individuals facing mental health challenges. Instead of targeting or stigmatizing them, it is crucial that we extend our support and understanding during their difficult times. By doing so, we can help create an environment where they feel accepted and valued. Open conversation, support, and love can help them transcend this boundary and help them feel like they are valuable, just like their peers. In addition, promoting mental health education and awareness in schools, workplaces, and communities is crucial. Providing accurate information about mental health, its impact, and available resources can help dispel myths and empower individuals to seek help and support when needed. Encouraging mental health screenings, regular check-ins, and providing accessible mental health services can contribute to a society that prioritizes well-being and addresses mental health issues proactively. Every member of society holds inherent value, including individuals experiencing mental health challenges. Removing stigma and providing support requires advocating for mental health, engaging in open conversations, and demonstrating love and support. By recognizing the worth and potential of all individuals, we foster an environment that values and supports the mental well-being of each person, allowing them to thrive alongside their peers.

Lack of Confidence

Overview

Teenagers, in the process of growing up, often fall victim to confidence and self-esteem issues. These stem from the fact that their body is changing right in front of their eyes, and they can do nothing about it. Weight gain is one of the major reasons why teenagers develop self-esteem issues. They start believing they are different and less valuable than their peers. Once they start believing this, they begin isolating and cutting them off. Sooner or later, they stop talking to people entirely, choosing not to communicate with anyone. They develop confidence issues as they do not believe that when they do talk to other people, they will not be made fun of. Isolation, coupled with such dark views of oneself, can give birth to dark thoughts in the brains of teenagers who are going through such a situation. They find ways of harming themselves, and since they do not talk to other people, they never reach out for help and end up fulfilling their dark mission, ending their life too early.

Solution

Teenagers should realize that going through the process of puberty is a normal thing. What one person's views are on them does not matter as they are more than their body. Teenagers often do not realize how their words can affect someone else. Teenagers need to realize that they need to be more accepting and supportive of their peers. Teenagers might believe that people will not talk to them, but that is not true. The first step is usually the hardest. They should try and get out of their comfort zone. Sparking up a conversation might seem like a challenging task, but a simple conversation starter about a mutual interest can help them make friends and lose the feeling of being lonely. Parents need to play an active role. If their child fails to make friends or is being bullied, they should step in and talk to their teen or go as far as to seek professional help from a therapist to avoid a dark fate.

Conclusion

Confidence issues can develop early in life. They might stem from various reasons, but parents need to play their responsibility and check if their child is struggling. They can seek professional help if they feel like their child is not responding well to their conversations. As children grow into teenagers, the societal pressures and expectations they face can intensify. They may begin comparing themselves to others, focusing heavily on their physical appearance, or seeking validation from external sources. It is crucial for teenagers to realize that their worth extends far beyond superficial measures. Encouraging self-acceptance, resilience, and a positive mindset can empower teenagers to recognize and embrace their inherent value, allowing them to navigate life's challenges with confidence and self-assurance.

Lack of Access to Healthy Food or Clean Water

Overview

As discussed above earlier in the book, it is necessary for teenagers to have a diet that contains all the crucial elements that are required for them to grow. In many instances, teenagers do not have access to healthy food and sources of clean water. Their physical well-being is directly dependent on this. However, failure to find the necessary resources will lead to their physical health being directly impacted. Consumption of unhealthy food and unclean water will lead to their immune system being compromised. This makes them susceptible to numerous diseases. The lack of such resources usually takes place in societies with high economic disparity. So, teenagers might feel hopeless and frustrated. This affects their mental health and might even lead to isolation due to fear of judgment. These dark thoughts can form and manifest into suicidal thoughts in the brain of a teenager who finds himself in such a situation.

Solution

The solution that will have the most major impact on this problem is to strengthen community support systems. Establishing charities can help bridge the gap between the rich and the poor and reduce economic disparity. This will ensure that everyone has access to the basic necessities of life. In addition, this will also ensure that people have access to medical care so no one who is suffering from diseases is rooted in the problem of lacking access to a clean water supply and unhealthy food. Providing care for mental health can further help reduce the number of suicides that occur due to this reason. It is important that the issue of socioeconomic disparity is addressed. Work towards reducing socioeconomic disparities and improving access to basic resources such as healthy food, clean water, education, and employment opportunities. Foster collaborations between healthcare providers and educational institutions can help introduce an effective approach to helping those in need. In order to help those who may be experiencing suicidal thoughts, it is important to train educators, healthcare providers, and community members to detect the indicators. Set up emergency hotlines and helplines for people in trouble. Create all-encompassing plans for preventing suicide, with an emphasis on early intervention, risk assessment, and specific help for those most at risk.

Conclusion

It is important to address this issue, as this is an issue of basic human rights. Everyone deserves the right to access healthy food and a source of clean water. People who are not provided with these resources fall victim to diseases that they do not have access to the medication to treat the diseases. People can join hands to help those in need. Charities and support programs can be set up for people who are in a situation that they see virtually no way out of. Food drives can be a great way to donate healthy food to people who do not have access to healthy food. This eradicates the chance that they will fall victim to malnutrition and, eventually, disease. Consequently, it lowers the chance that they will commit suicide because humanity failed them.

Feeling Trapped or Stuck in Life

Overview

Feeling trapped or stuck in life can be an overwhelming experience for teenagers. Puberty brings about a multitude of physical, emotional, and social changes that can be difficult to navigate. Adolescents often struggle with their evolving identities, grappling with questions of self-worth, belonging, and purpose. When faced with these internal conflicts, coupled with external pressures, they may feel like they are drowning in their struggles. In some cases, teenagers turn to unhealthy coping mechanisms such as substance abuse, self-harm, or self-isolation, further exacerbating their sense of being trapped. These destructive behaviors can reinforce their belief that their life will never change and that they are destined for a future filled with despair. Moreover, the limited options and opportunities available to teenagers can contribute to their feelings of hopelessness. They may perceive that they have few avenues for personal growth, education, or career prospects. This perceived lack of future prospects intensifies their belief that they are doomed to failure, perpetuating the idea that their life will never improve. The pressure to fit in socially can also intensify the feeling of being trapped. Teenagers often have a strong desire to be accepted by their peers, and when they feel like they don't belong or that they are unable to meet societal expectations, it can lead to deep-seated feelings of isolation and alienation. The idea of a life filled with rejection and loneliness can be unbearable, further reinforcing the belief that suicide is the only escape from this perpetual cycle of suffering.

Solution

Teens who believe they have nowhere to go in life require multifaceted forms of help and intervention. First and foremost, it is critical that adolescents have access to mental health services. They can find acceptance, assistance, and the opportunity to build coping skills via counseling, therapy, and support groups at school and in the community. By removing the stigma associated with talking about mental health, we can assist young people in realizing they are not alone in their experiences of difficulty. Teenagers rely heavily on their relatives and parents for encouragement and support. Teenagers will feel more comfortable opening up to their loved ones about their struggles and asking for advice if they are provided with an atmosphere of open communication, strengthened family dynamics, and a supportive environment. It's also helpful to provide parents with information and tools they may use to better their own parenting practices and encourage them to learn more about mental health. The promotion of mental health education requires extensive educational campaigns and awareness activities. Efforts like this may dispel myths, make people more aware of warning indicators, and boost support for intervening early. Greater awareness of mental health difficulties, the acquisition of coping skills, and the cultivation of empathy towards peers may all be achieved by incorporating mental health education into school curricula and offering tools for instructors.

Teen suicide is a community problem that needs everyone's attention. Educators, medical professionals, civic leaders, and lawmakers must work together on this. By pooling resources, coordinating efforts, and developing a holistic strategy together, much may be accomplished. Awareness events, volunteer programs, and peer support networks are all examples of community-driven activities that may help teens feel less alone. Building a society where people can and do care for one another and accept one another is also essential. Teens' emotional health may be greatly improved by encouraging acts of kindness, compassion, and acceptance in the classroom, the neighborhood, and the virtual world. Adolescents might feel less isolated and have more of a support system by engaging in constructive social interactions and cultivating a sense of belonging.

Conclusion

In conclusion, addressing the issue of teenagers feeling trapped or stuck in life and reducing suicide rates among adolescents requires a comprehensive and collaborative approach. By providing mental health services, improving family relationships, disseminating information on mental health, and cultivating a caring community, we can create a more positive environment that supports the well-being of teenagers and helps them navigate through their challenges.

Feeling Like a Burden to Others

Overview

A sense of being a burden on others has been linked to a number of teen suicides. Teens who suffer from this perspective worry that their loved ones are being overburdened by their presence or their difficulties. Teenagers with mental health issues, including depression, anxiety, or bipolar disorder, may feel guilty about their illness because they don't want to be a burden on their loved ones. They could feel guilty and like a burden on their loved ones because they think their loved ones have to continually worry about them or take care of them. Teens who are going through difficult times in their relationships, whether it be with friends, love partners, or members of their own family, may feel responsible for the pressure and believe that their presence adds to the load that others are already carrying. The intensity of feelings of guilt and self-blame can be amplified when there are issues in a relationship. Consequently, when adolescents do not have access to a support structure that recognizes or comprehends the challenges they face, they may have the experience of being alone and a burden on others.

Solution

An all-encompassing and compassionate strategy is needed to address the problem of teens feeling like a burden. Teenagers can benefit from having honest conversations with trusted adults, including parents, teachers, and friends. Make sure they have somewhere they can talk about their problems without worrying about being misunderstood or rejected. Encourage caring interactions characterized by attentive listening and compassionate thought. Make sure that young people may easily get in touch with mental health services, including therapy, counseling, and support groups. They can learn to cope with their mental health challenges and get the treatment they need from these programs. Reduce stigma and increase opportunities for early intervention by spreading information about mental health. Give teens a voice by equipping them with appropriate coping strategies and methods for building resilience. Methods of dealing with stress, methods of addressing problems, self-care routines, and methods of controlling one's emotions all fall under this category. By giving them these resources, we empower them to face adversity with confidence. Give teens a voice by equipping them with appropriate coping strategies and methods for building resilience. Methods of dealing with stress, methods of addressing problems, self-care routines, and methods of controlling one's emotions all fall under this category. By giving them these resources, we empower them to face adversity with confidence. Using the aforementioned techniques. One can help teenagers that are going through a difficult time believing that they are a burden to others around them.

Conclusion

It is essential to be aware of the fact that these impressions cannot correspond to the actual circumstances of the scenario. On the other hand, for adolescents who are going through this experience, the weight that they feel is quite real and extremely unpleasant. It is essential to provide them with support and empathy, as well as comfort, in their time of need. Their emotions of being a burden can be alleviated, and the risk of suicide can be reduced if they are encouraged to communicate in an open and nonjudgmental manner, if they seek professional assistance, and if they are surrounded by people who are supportive of them.

Self-Criticism

Overview

Teens who are victims of self-criticism often suffer from image issues stemming from a lack of confidence. These teenagers have to feel neglected and believe they are fundamentally flawed and unworthy. This leads to unhealthy obsessions being created to be perfect, falling into peer pressure, and acting in ways that are uncharacteristic of them. They become obsessed with the idea of being perfect and start doing things to achieve it. They develop more issues this way as they slowly realize what they had believed would be a good strategy to solve their issues is actually not good at all. They often start being bullied by their peers and get socially rejected. In turn, this leads to self-critical thoughts being developed. Often, it is too late by the time the victim realizes and believes suicide is their only option; and they end up losing their life.

Solution

A teenager going through such a scenario may find that talking to a therapist is an effective method to avoid being a victim of such a tragic outcome. As soon as this issue presents itself, it is essential to look for assistance from a qualified specialist. Going to counseling in order to get guidance on how to go in life is something that may benefit a person. When a parent learns about a challenge that their child is going through, it is critical for them to step in and take control of the situation themselves. A guardian can provide a sense of security in their adolescent charge by assuring them that they are worthwhile and important.

During this trying period, it is essential to have support services available for mental health. This contributes to the guarantee that they are adequately geared up to charter through this unfamiliar region. The development of healthy self-esteem in adolescents can motivate them to participate in activities that they find enjoyable, which, in turn, can assist them in acquiring the self-assurance that they may be lacking. In addition, this can help individuals deal with stressful situations, disappointments, and negative thoughts about themselves. This can be of further assistance in regulating feelings and promoting activities that encourage self-care. It is imperative that adolescents understand that they are worthwhile and that they play an important role in the world. They should be aware that they are excellent just as they are, and they should seek to better themselves at a speed that they find appropriate. They should not be concerned with what other people in society may think of them, but rather they should focus on improving themselves.

Conclusion

Because of the unnecessarily high expectations that have been established by society, a significant number of adolescents struggle with difficulties related to self-criticism. This raging fire is fueled by the fact that adolescents are frequently judged in comparison to their contemporaries, which encourages adolescents to feel that they will never be able to live up to the potential that they possess. They frequently lack the courage to ask for help because they are concerned that others would view them as less capable than their contemporaries if they did so. They don't let anyone know how they feel and don't ask for assistance since they bottle up their feelings. It's common for parents and guardians to be woefully unaware of the struggles their children are facing. Teenagers end up committing suicide as a result of the concern that they are not as excellent as their friends, which leads to the development of self-criticism difficulties in these adolescents.

Major Accident, Natural Disaster, or Assault

Overview

Puberty is a period of time when the body goes through drastic changes. Hence, it is difficult for the brain to regulate emotions effectively. It is due to the fact that the brain is undergoing the process of developing properly. Consequently, when a situation occurs where a person going through the process of puberty has to experience emotions and loss, they often fail to process emotions in a way that they can grow from it. Incidents such as major accidents, natural disasters, and assaults are all examples of a situation where teenagers might feel like they have experienced an emotion that they find difficult to process. Therefore, they believe that they will never be able to grow from it. Reeling from such a major loss, they think that there is no point in living ahead of the point in time that they are in. Under this impression, dark thoughts start forming in their brains. More often than not, they act out on these dark thoughts and put an early to their life, a life that was important for them to experience to their potential.

Solution

For the sake of public safety, it is essential for the government to establish crisis response centers in the event that severe catastrophes occur. The existence of these centers will guarantee that individuals are assisted through important interventions in a manner that is both successful and helps them process it in a healthy manner. This will be the case since the presence of these centers will ensure this. They should be given assistance and support while they go through such trying times since, in many circumstances, the loss of a significant person or item can cause them to feel that they will never, ever be able to get it back in their lifetime. These people should be given such assistance and support. They have false beliefs, such as the notion that they would never be able to rebuild their home after it was destroyed by a natural disaster. In a circumstance like this, it is imperative that the government step in and ensure that they have access to the requirements for survival. In addition to this, they fear that the money they would have to pay for their medical care will be an obligation that they will be unable to repay under any circumstances. Because of this, it is critical that everyone have access to affordable or even free medical care. Additionally, those who are reeling from the impact of such a significant loss should have easy access to professional counseling services.

Conclusion

It is impossible for a person to adequately prepare for unanticipated events such as a natural disaster, a significant accident, or an assault. Because of this, there is no feasible strategy that can be put into action in the event that a scenario like this one arises. It is essential that the government fulfill its responsibility of ensuring the populace that they would not be abandoned to fend for themselves in such a circumstance. Many people, particularly adolescents who do not know how to effectively process the situation, really think that they will never recover from such a loss, and this is especially true in circumstances when the person believes that they will never heal from the loss. There should be specialized facilities that are pre-prepared to handle any type of emergency by having all of the necessary supplies on hand at all times. In the event that someone has suffered such a significant loss, they should be offered free medical treatment and counseling sessions so that they may concentrate on finding healthy ways to cope with the circumstance rather than letting it take their life. This will prevent the scenario from being the cause of their suicide.

Cancer

Overview

Cancer is a disease that plagues people of all ages. While it is not a disease that is prevalent among the youth, it still poses a threat to children of people who have a family history of cancer. Every year, a small number of children are diagnosed with cancer. The most common types of cancer in teens include leukemia, lymphoma, brain and central nervous system tumors, bone tumors, and germ cell tumors. The symptoms of cancer in teens can vary depending on the type and stage of cancer. Nonetheless, the information that a person is suffering from cancer is a hard pill to swallow. Teens, with their undeveloped brains, find it difficult to process. Cancer can change their body further, which can lead to more confidence issues and make them see themselves in a different light, one that makes them feel worse about themselves. What they don't realize is that they still have a life that they need to live to the fullest. They often commit suicide, deciding not to live a life of pain and agony.

Solution

The most important thing to do to tackle this issue is to raise awareness. Teenagers need to be informed that a cancer diagnosis does not necessarily mean that their life is going to come to an end. While the length and outcome of their life may depend on factors such as the stage and type of cancer, they need to be reminded that they still serve a purpose and can find strength and support in their journey. It is crucial that parents take on the responsibility of comforting their children through this time of turmoil, providing them with love, understanding, and reassurance. Letting them know that they are not alone in their fight is essential in helping them navigate the challenges they may face. Teenagers need to realize the fact that the advancements in medicine and oncology mean that there is a high probability of successful treatment and survival. The medical field has made remarkable progress in understanding and treating cancer with improved diagnostic techniques, targeted therapies, and personalized treatment approaches. It is important to emphasize the importance of seeking timely medical attention, following recommended screening guidelines, and advocating for their own healthcare needs. Moreover, raising awareness among the general population, including schools, communities, and the media, is vital. Support networks and resources should be readily available for teenagers and their families. This includes access to specialized healthcare providers, pediatric oncologists, and support groups tailored to the unique needs of teen cancer patients. Psychosocial support, counseling services, and mental health resources should be integral parts of the care provided to address the emotional and psychological challenges that often accompany a cancer diagnosis. Additionally, efforts should be made to integrate education and support systems within schools to ensure continuity in education during treatment and to provide a supportive environment for teen cancer survivors as they transition back into their academic lives.

Conclusion

It doesn't matter how old a person is; cancer can take their life at any time. However, it is essential to remember that we are in control, not cancer. Anyone afflicted with cancer must have hope and combat the disease. The importance of reminding those who are suffering that they are not alone in their anguish cannot be overstated. Teens are vulnerable and lack the resources an adult would have, so it's important that they know their loved ones are doing everything they can to save them. It's also important to reassure them that their contributions are still appreciated and needed. Instead of thinking that cancer has all the cards and they're doomed, they should be encouraged to enjoy each day to the utmost. Taking your own life is never the best choice. It is important for teens to fight to survive.

Sexual Orientation and Gender Identity Issues

Overview

Sexual orientation and gender identity issues are complex and multifaceted. These issues are not new, but they have become increasingly visible in recent years. People who identify as LGBTQ+ face discrimination, harassment, and violence due to their sexual orientation or gender identity, which can have serious consequences for their mental health. This can include an increased risk of suicide, among other mental health problems.

Sexual orientation and gender identity refer to a person's attraction to others and how they identify themselves in terms of gender. Historically, people who identified as LGBTQ+ have been marginalized and discriminated against. Despite some progress, there is still a lot of discrimination and stigma that these individuals face. This can lead to mental health problems, including depression, anxiety, and suicidal thoughts.

The discrimination and stigma that LGBTQ+ individuals face can take many forms. For example, they may face bullying at school or in the workplace, exclusion from social events, or even violence. This can lead to feelings of isolation, shame, and low self-esteem, which can contribute to mental health problems.

The causes of sexual orientation and gender identity issues are not fully understood. Some theories suggest that biological factors, such as genetics and hormones, may play a role. Others suggest that environmental factors, such as upbringing and socialization, may also contribute to these issues.

Research has shown that LGBTQ+ individuals are more likely to experience mental health problems compared to the general population. This is due in part to the discrimination and stigma that they face. LGBTQ+ individuals are also more likely to experience traumatic events, such as hate crimes or sexual assault, which can contribute to mental health problems.

People who identify as LGBTQ+ face a higher risk of suicide compared to the general population. This is due to a combination of factors, including discrimination, harassment, and violence. LGBTQ+ individuals are also more likely to experience mental health problems, such as depression and anxiety, which can increase the risk of suicide.

According to the Trevor Project, a national organization that provides crisis intervention and suicide prevention services to LGBTQ+ youth, suicide is the second leading cause of death among young people ages 10-24. LGBTQ+ youth are four times more likely to attempt suicide than their heterosexual peers.

Solution

The solution to sexual orientation and gender identity issues is to promote acceptance and tolerance. This can be done through education and awareness campaigns, as well as through policy changes that protect LGBTQ+ individuals from discrimination and harassment. Mental health services should also be made more accessible to LGBTQ+ individuals who may be struggling with mental health problems.

Education and awareness campaigns can help to reduce discrimination and stigma towards LGBTQ+ individuals. This can include educating people about the harmful effects of discrimination and encouraging people to be more accepting of those who are different from themselves. Policy changes can also help to protect LGBTQ+ individuals from discrimination and harassment. For example, laws can be put in place to prevent discrimination in the workplace or in housing.

Mental health services should be made more accessible to LGBTQ+ individuals who may be struggling with mental health problems. This can include providing LGBTQ+ individuals with access to mental health professionals who are trained to work with their specific needs. Mental health services should also be affordable and available in a variety of settings, such as schools and community centers.

Conclusion

Sexual orientation and gender identity issues are complex and multifaceted. While progress has been made in recent years, there is still a long way to go in terms of promoting acceptance and tolerance. By working together, we can create a world where LGBTQ+ individuals are treated with respect and dignity and where mental health services are available to those who need them. It is important to continue the conversation about sexual orientation and gender identity issues and to work towards a future where everyone is treated equally, regardless of their sexual orientation or gender identity.

Religious And Cultural Conflicts

Overview

Religious and cultural conflicts can cause immense psychological distress, which can contribute to suicidal ideation or thoughts of suicide. These conflicts can arise between individuals within the same religious group or culture or between individuals from different cultural or religious backgrounds. When a person's beliefs and values are questioned or threatened, it can lead to a crisis of identity, loss of hope, and feelings of isolation and despair. In some cases, these intense emotions can lead to suicidal thoughts and behaviors.

Religious and cultural conflicts can have a significant impact on mental health. Studies have shown that such conflicts can lead to depression, anxiety, and other mental health issues. These conflicts can also lead to feelings of shame and guilt, which can contribute to suicidal ideation.

The causes of religious and cultural conflicts are complex and multifaceted. In some cases, these conflicts arise due to differences in values, beliefs, and practices between individuals or groups. In other cases, religious and cultural conflicts may arise due to misunderstandings or stereotypes about different cultures or religions.

In some cases, religious and cultural conflicts may be exacerbated by political, economic, or social factors. For example, economic inequality or political instability may fuel religious and cultural conflicts by creating a sense of competition or a need to protect one's own group or identity.

Furthermore, the impact of globalization and increasing multiculturalism can lead to increased encounters and interactions between individuals from different cultural or religious backgrounds. These encounters can lead to conflicts, particularly if individuals are not equipped with the skills and knowledge to navigate and appreciate cultural differences.

Solutions

To address religious and cultural conflicts, there are several solutions that individuals, organizations, and communities can implement.

Education and Dialogue

Education and dialogue are among the most effective solutions to religious and cultural conflicts. This can involve promoting greater understanding and respect for different beliefs and values through interfaith dialogues, multicultural events, and other community-based initiatives. Education and dialogue can help individuals develop the skills and knowledge to navigate cultural differences and build bridges of understanding and empathy.

Mental Health Support and Counseling Services

Individuals experiencing distress related to religious and cultural conflicts can benefit from mental health support and counseling services. Mental health professionals can help individuals work through their emotions and develop coping strategies to manage stress and anxiety. Suicide prevention hotlines and crisis support services can also provide immediate assistance and support for individuals who are experiencing suicidal ideation or other mental health crises related to religious and cultural conflicts.

Creating Safe Spaces

Creating safe spaces for individuals to express their concerns and share their experiences can also be helpful in addressing religious and cultural conflicts. This can involve creating forums for discussion and debate, as well as creating spaces where individuals can feel safe to express their thoughts and feelings without fear of judgment or persecution.

Encouraging Diversity and Inclusion

Organizations and communities can play an active role in addressing religious and cultural conflicts by promoting diversity and inclusion. This can involve creating policies and practices that promote diversity and inclusion, as well as actively working to address discrimination and bias. By promoting diversity and inclusion, individuals from different cultural and religious backgrounds can feel valued and respected, which can help reduce tensions and conflicts.

Advocating for Social Justice

Religious and cultural conflicts can be exacerbated by social injustice, inequality, and discrimination. Advocating for social justice can help address some of the root causes of religious and cultural conflicts. This can involve working to address economic inequality, promoting human rights, and advocating for policies that promote equality and justice.

Conclusion

Religious and cultural conflicts can have serious consequences for mental health, including an increased risk of suicidal ideation. It is important to approach these conflicts with empathy and understanding and to provide mental health support and crisis services to those in need.

By working together to promote greater understanding and respect for diverse beliefs and values, we can help reduce the risk of suicide and promote greater mental health and well-being for all. It is important to recognize that religious and cultural conflicts are complex and multifaceted issues that require ongoing attention and effort to address effectively.

Organizations and communities can actively address religious and cultural conflicts by promoting education and dialogue, creating safe spaces for individuals to express their concerns, and encouraging diversity and inclusion. By working together to address the root causes of religious and cultural conflicts, we can create a more peaceful and harmonious society where individuals of all backgrounds can thrive.

Family Conflict and Estrangement

Overview

Family conflict and estrangement are complex issues that can cause a variety of negative outcomes for individuals and families. One of the most serious consequences is the increased risk of suicide. Feelings of loneliness, hopelessness, and despair can be overwhelming when family members are not on good terms and can lead to suicidal thoughts and behaviors. This is why it is important to understand the underlying causes of family conflict and estrangement and work towards resolving them constructively.

Family conflict and estrangement can stem from a wide range of issues, including but not limited to unresolved past traumas, communication breakdowns, differences in values or beliefs, financial stress, and mental health concerns. It is important to identify the root causes of conflict and estrangement in order to effectively address them.

Solutions

There are a variety of solutions that can help address family conflict and estrangement and reduce the risk of suicide for individuals and families.

Seeking Professional Help

One solution is to seek the help of a therapist or mediator to facilitate communication and understanding among family members. A trained professional can help to identify the root causes of conflict and estrangement and develop a plan to resolve them. They can also offer guidance on how to communicate effectively and constructively with family members. Therapy and mediation can be a safe space for family members to express their emotions and concerns and to work toward healing and reconciliation.

Seeking Support from Loved Ones

Another solution is to seek support from friends or other loved ones who can provide emotional support and a sense of belonging. Having a strong support system can help individuals cope with the stress and emotions associated with family conflict and estrangement. Friends and loved ones can offer a listening ear, provide encouragement, and offer practical assistance. They can also help to reduce the isolation and loneliness that can contribute to suicidal thoughts and behaviors.

Joining Support Groups or Engaging in Activities

Joining support groups or engaging in activities that promote mental and emotional well-being can also be helpful. Support groups can provide a sense of community and belonging and offer a space to share experiences and learn from others. Engaging in activities that promote mental and emotional well-being, such as exercise or mindfulness meditation, can also help to reduce stress and promote positive mental health.

Resolving Issues and Building Healthier Relationships

Ultimately, the goal of addressing family conflict and estrangement is to resolve the underlying issues and build healthier relationships within families. This requires a willingness to communicate openly and honestly, to listen actively, and to practice empathy and understanding. By working together to address the root causes of conflict and estrangement, individuals and families can overcome the challenges and build stronger, more supportive relationships.

Conclusion

Family conflict and estrangement can be a serious issue that requires attention and effort to resolve. It is important to recognize the warning signs of suicidal thoughts and behaviors and to seek help if needed. By working together to address the underlying issues and providing support and resources, it is possible to overcome the challenges and build healthier relationships within families. Seeking professional help, seeking support from loved ones, joining support groups or engaging in activities, resolving issues, and building healthier relationships are all potential solutions to addressing family conflict and estrangement.

Fear of Punishment and Legal Consequences

Overview

Fear of punishment and legal consequences can be a significant stressor in an individual's life, leading to various mental health issues. It can also push someone to the point of suicide, especially if they are facing criminal charges or a prison sentence. The fear of being punished or facing legal consequences can be overwhelming, leading to feelings of hopelessness, helplessness, and despair. The fear of punishment and legal consequences can have severe and lasting impacts on an individual's mental health. Fear and anxiety can lead to depression, post-traumatic stress disorder, and other mental health conditions. It can also lead to physical health problems, such as high blood pressure, heart disease, and chronic pain. The legal system can be especially challenging for individuals who do not have access to legal resources or support. The fear of being caught up in a complicated legal system without adequate support can be overwhelming, leading to feelings of isolation and desperation.

Solution

To prevent fear of punishment and legal consequences from leading to suicide, it is essential to provide individuals with adequate legal support and counseling. This includes providing information about their legal rights, access to legal representation, and mental health resources. Providing access to legal support and counseling is crucial as it can help individuals navigate the legal system and reduce their fear of punishment and legal consequences. Access to legal support can also ensure that individuals receive fair treatment and are not subject to harsh or unjust punishment. Legal professionals, such as lawyers, can provide legal advice, representation, and advocacy to individuals who are facing legal challenges. In addition to legal support, mental health resources can also play a critical role in reducing the fear of punishment and legal consequences. Mental health support can help individuals manage the stress and anxiety associated with facing legal challenges. It can also provide individuals with coping strategies and tools to help them navigate the legal system. One approach that has been successful in addressing the fear of punishment and legal consequences is restorative justice. This approach focuses on repairing the harm caused by criminal behavior and restoring relationships between victims, offenders, and the community. Restorative justice can help reduce the fear of punishment and legal consequences by providing individuals with an opportunity to take responsibility for their actions and make amends. Another solution is to provide training and support to legal professionals and law enforcement officials. This can include training on mental health issues and how to recognize warning signs of suicide. By providing legal professionals with the tools and resources they need to support individuals facing legal challenges, we can help reduce the fear of punishment and legal consequences. In addition to providing legal support and counseling, it is also important to address the underlying factors that contribute to fear of punishment and legal consequences. This can include addressing poverty, lack of education, and systemic inequalities that can lead to individuals being caught up in the legal system. By addressing these underlying factors, we can reduce the number of individuals who are at risk of facing legal challenges and reduce the fear of punishment and legal consequences.

Conclusion

Fear of punishment and legal consequences is a complex issue that requires a multifaceted approach. By providing support and resources for individuals facing legal challenges, we can reduce the risk of suicide and promote better mental health outcomes. It is essential to reduce the stigma associated with seeking help for mental health issues and to provide adequate legal support and counseling. By working together to address this issue, we can create a legal system that is more compassionate, supportive, and understanding of the mental health needs of individuals facing legal challenges. Reducing the fear of punishment and legal consequences is not only essential for promoting better mental health outcomes, but it is also crucial for creating a more just and equitable society. By addressing the underlying factors that contribute to fear of punishment and legal consequences, we can create a legal system that is fair and just for all. By promoting restorative justice and providing legal support and counseling, we can help individuals facing legal challenges find a way forward that is compassionate and supportive.

Physical disabilities or limitations

Overview

Physical disabilities or limitations can have a profound and long-lasting impact on an individual's mental health and well-being. Living with a physical disability can be an isolating experience that can lead to feelings of disempowerment, frustration, and hopelessness. These limitations can create barriers to carrying out daily tasks, participating in social activities, and achieving personal goals, which can contribute to mental health issues such as anxiety and depression. The emotional impact of living with a physical disability can be further compounded by social stigma, discrimination, and lack of access to supportive resources. The link between physical disabilities, mental health, and suicide The emotional and psychological toll of living with a physical disability can be immense and can contribute to an increased risk of suicide. Research has shown that individuals with physical disabilities are at a higher risk of suicide than the general population. The reasons for this are complex and can include a lack of social support, low self-esteem, and feelings of worthlessness. Additionally, individuals with physical disabilities may face a range of challenges, including financial insecurity, a lack of access to healthcare, and physical pain, which can increase their risk of developing mental health issues.

Solution

Providing individuals with the resources and support they need to manage their disabilities or limitations is critical. Medical care, rehabilitation, assistive devices, and counseling services all play a vital role in helping individuals cope with their physical disabilities. However, it is also necessary to recognize that individuals with physical disabilities have unique needs that require tailored solutions. For instance, individuals with mobility issues may require accessible transportation or housing. Additionally, it is essential to create opportunities for individuals with physical disabilities to participate in social activities, access community resources, and achieve personal goals. This can help combat the feelings of isolation and disempowerment that may contribute to mental health issues. For example, community centers can offer inclusive programs that cater to the specific needs of individuals with physical disabilities, such as adaptive sports or recreational activities. It is also crucial to raise awareness around disability and mental health issues, reduce stigma, and promote inclusivity. This can be achieved through advocacy, education, and community outreach. By providing individuals with the support and resources they need, we can help reduce the risk of suicide and improve the overall well-being of those living with disabilities or limitations. It is equally important to address the systemic barriers that individuals with physical disabilities face. This includes ensuring that individuals have access to affordable healthcare, employment opportunities, and social services. By reducing these barriers, we can help create a more inclusive and supportive society for individuals with physical disabilities. For example, employers can provide reasonable accommodations for employees with physical disabilities, such as flexible work hours or assistive technology.

Conclusion

Physical disabilities or limitations can be a contributing factor to suicide. However, by addressing the emotional and social impact of physical disabilities and providing individuals with the support and resources they need, we can help reduce the risk of suicide and improve the mental health and well-being of individuals living with disabilities or limitations. It is crucial to provide individuals with the resources, support, and care they need, as well as raise awareness and reduce stigma around disability and mental health issues. By doing so, we can work towards a more inclusive and supportive society that values the contributions of all individuals, regardless of their physical abilities or limitations.

Difficulty managing anger and frustration

Overview

Difficulty managing anger or frustration is a serious issue that affects many individuals. Anger is a natural human emotion that can help us respond to threatening situations, but when it becomes intense or uncontrollable, it can lead to negative consequences. People who have difficulty managing their anger or frustration can often experience intense feelings of anger that are difficult to control, leading to aggressive or violent behavior towards themselves or others. This can ultimately result in a sense of hopelessness and despair, which may lead to suicidal thoughts or actions. Causes of Difficulty Managing Anger or Frustration There are many factors that can contribute to difficulty managing anger or frustration. For some people, it may be related to a medical condition, such as a brain injury or hormonal imbalance. For others, it may be related to a history of trauma or abuse, which can lead to intense feelings of anger or frustration. Substance abuse, stress, and poor communication skills can also contribute to difficulty managing anger.

Consequences of Difficulty Managing Anger or Frustration The consequences of difficulty managing anger or frustration can be severe. Individuals who struggle with anger or frustration may experience problems in their personal and professional relationships. They may also experience physical health problems, such as high blood pressure, heart disease, and chronic pain. In addition, difficulty managing anger or frustration can lead to mental health problems, such as anxiety, depression, and post-traumatic stress disorder (PTSD). The most serious consequence of difficulty managing anger or frustration is suicide.

Solution

There are several evidence-based treatments available for individuals who have difficulty managing anger or frustration. One of the most effective treatments is cognitive-behavioral therapy (CBT), which helps individuals identify and change negative thought patterns and behaviors that contribute to anger and frustration. In CBT, individuals learn healthy coping mechanisms and strategies for managing their emotions, which can help reduce the frequency and intensity of angry outbursts. Another effective treatment for difficulty managing anger or frustration is anger management therapy. This type of therapy is designed to help individuals understand the root causes of their anger and learn how to manage it in healthier ways. Anger management therapy typically involves teaching individuals how to identify triggers that cause anger, how to control physical responses to anger (such as increased heart rate and rapid breathing), and how to communicate their feelings effectively. In addition to therapy, there are several self-help strategies that individuals can use to manage their anger and frustration. One of the most effective self-help strategies is practicing relaxation techniques, such as deep breathing, meditation, and progressive muscle relaxation. These techniques can help individuals calm down and reduce the intensity of angry feelings. Another self-help strategy is engaging in physical activity. Exercise has been shown to reduce stress and anxiety, which can help individuals manage their anger and frustration more effectively. Engaging in physical activity also helps release endorphins, which can improve mood and reduce feelings of anger. Finally, it is important for individuals with difficulty managing anger or frustration to avoid triggers that may lead to angry outbursts. This may involve avoiding certain situations or people that tend to cause anger or learning how to respond to these triggers in a more positive way. Overall, the most effective approach to managing anger or frustration is likely to be a combination of therapy and self-help strategies. By seeking help and support, individuals can develop the skills and strategies they need to manage their emotions and prevent negative consequences such as suicide.

Conclusion

Difficulty managing anger or frustration can have serious consequences, including suicide. However, there are effective treatments available that can help individuals manage their emotions and prevent suicide. It is important to seek help if you are struggling with anger or frustration and to remember that there is hope for recovery. With the right support and treatment, individuals can learn to manage their emotions and lead fulfilling lives. It is important to reach out to professionals, friends, or family members for help and support. By taking action to address difficulty managing anger or frustration, individuals can improve their mental and physical health, as well as their relationships with others.

Lack of access to legal representation or advocacy

Overview

Suicide is a complex issue that can have many underlying causes, including mental illness, social isolation, financial difficulties, and relationship problems. However, one factor that is often overlooked but can be a significant contributor to suicide risk is the lack of access to legal representation or advocacy.

When individuals are unable to access legal assistance or advocacy, they may feel helpless and trapped in challenging situations, leading to feelings of hopelessness and despair. This can be particularly true for those who are facing legal challenges that impact their livelihood or well-being, such as eviction from their home, loss of custody of their children, or discrimination in the workplace.

Research has shown that individuals who are involved in legal disputes are at an increased risk of suicide, particularly when they are unable to access the legal resources they need to protect their rights and interests. For example, a study published in the Journal of Epidemiology and Community Health found that people who were involved in legal disputes related to housing or employment were more likely to die by suicide than those who were not involved in legal disputes.

Solution

One solution to the problem of lack of access to legal representation or advocacy is the provision of legal aid services. These services can help individuals who are unable to afford legal representation or advocacy. Legal aid services can provide assistance with a range of legal issues, including housing, employment, family law, and immigration.

Legal aid services are often provided by non-profit organizations, government agencies, and private law firms. They can be funded through a variety of sources, including grants, donations, and government funding. Legal aid services can help individuals navigate the legal system, understand their rights, and access the legal resources they need to protect their interests.

Another important solution is to increase awareness about the impact that legal challenges can have on mental health and suicide risk. Many people may not be aware of the connection between legal problems and suicide and may not seek help until it is too late. By increasing awareness and providing education about this issue, we can help to prevent suicide and ensure that individuals are able to access the legal resources they need to protect their well-being.

In addition to legal aid services, there are many organizations that provide advocacy services to individuals who are facing legal challenges, such as discrimination, harassment, or abuse. These organizations can help individuals navigate the legal system, connect them with appropriate legal resources, and provide emotional support during what can be a very difficult time. Advocacy services can also help individuals understand their rights and make informed decisions about legal matters.

Ultimately, addressing the problem of lack of access to legal representation or advocacy requires a collaborative effort between legal professionals, mental health providers, and community advocates to ensure that everyone has access to the support they need to protect their rights and mental health. By working together, we can help to prevent suicide and support individuals who are facing challenging circumstances.

Conclusion

Lack of access to legal representation or advocacy is a significant problem that can contribute to feelings of hopelessness and despair, which may ultimately lead to suicide. It is important to recognize the impact that legal challenges can have on individuals and to provide access to legal assistance and advocacy, particularly for those who are most vulnerable. By doing so, we can help to prevent suicide and support individuals who are facing challenging circumstances. Ultimately, addressing this issue requires a collaborative effort between legal professionals, mental health providers, and community advocates to ensure that everyone has access to the support they need to protect their rights and mental health.

Lack of meaning or fulfillment in life

Overview

Lack of meaning or fulfillment in life is a multifaceted issue that affects millions of people worldwide. It can be caused by various factors, including a lack of a sense of purpose, dissatisfaction with one's career, personal life, or relationships, or a feeling of disconnection from others. This sense of emptiness and lack of direction can lead to a deep sense of despair and hopelessness, which in turn can contribute to suicide.

People experiencing a lack of meaning or fulfillment in life may feel stuck in a rut, unsure of how to find purpose and fulfillment. This can lead to a cycle of negative thoughts and emotions that can be difficult to break. However, there are many strategies that individuals can use to combat these feelings and find greater meaning and purpose in their lives.

One significant aspect of this issue is the increasing prevalence of burnout in the modern workplace. With the rise of remote work and the blurring of work-life boundaries, many people are experiencing a sense of disconnection from their work and a lack of purpose. This is often exacerbated by the pressure to be constantly productive and the feeling that one's work is never done.

Solution

Seek Out New Experiences and Challenges

One effective way to combat feelings of emptiness and lack of direction is to try new experiences and take on new challenges. This could mean taking up a new hobby or pursuing a passion that has been neglected in the past. By pushing oneself outside of their comfort zone, individuals can gain a sense of accomplishment and purpose.

To seek out new experiences, individuals can make a list of things they have always wanted to do or try. It could be something as simple as trying a new restaurant or as big as traveling to a new country. By setting goals and taking steps towards achieving them, individuals can gain a sense of direction and a feeling of purpose.

Focus on Gratitude and Appreciation

Another approach is to focus on building a sense of gratitude and appreciation for the good things in life. One way to do this is by keeping a daily gratitude journal, in which an individual writes down three things they are thankful for each day. By focusing on the positive aspects of life, it is possible to shift one's perspective and gain a greater sense of purpose and fulfillment.

In addition to keeping a gratitude journal, individuals can practice mindfulness and meditation to help them focus on the present moment and appreciate what they have. By taking time to reflect on the good things in life, individuals can develop a more positive outlook and a greater sense of fulfillment.

Seek Social Connections and Support

Social connections and support are also important in finding greater meaning and fulfillment in life. This might involve joining a community group, club, or other social activity. By connecting with others who share similar interests and values, individuals can build a sense of belonging and purpose.

To seek social connections, individuals can look for local events or groups that align with their interests. They can also reach out to friends and family members to schedule regular social activities or gatherings. By building a supportive network of people, individuals can feel more connected and fulfilled.

Prioritize Self-Care and Mental Health

It is essential to take care of oneself by prioritizing self-care and mental health. This could involve practicing mindfulness, getting adequate sleep and exercise, and seeking out therapy or counseling if needed. By taking care of oneself, it is possible to build resilience and better cope with the challenges of life.

To prioritize self-care, individuals can make a self-care plan that includes activities or practices that help them feel relaxed and rejuvenated. This could include taking a warm bath, going for a walk in nature, or practicing yoga. By making self-care a priority, individuals can build a stronger foundation for their overall well-being.

Seek Professional Help

If feelings of emptiness and lack of meaning persist, it is important to seek out professional help. A mental health professional can provide support, guidance, and treatment options to help individuals cope with these difficult emotions.

Individuals can seek professional help by talking to their primary care physician or by searching for mental health professionals in their area. By reaching out for help, individuals can get the support they need to find greater meaning and fulfillment in life.

Conclusion

In conclusion, a lack of meaning or fulfillment in life is a serious issue that can contribute to suicide. However, by taking proactive steps to address these feelings and seeking out professional help when needed, individuals can regain a sense of purpose and find greater fulfillment in their lives. It is important to remember that you are not alone, and there is always help available if you need it. By seeking out new experiences, focusing on gratitude and appreciation, building social connections, and seeking out professional help when needed, it is possible to find greater meaning and purpose in life.

Lack of meaning or fulfillment in life is a serious issue that can have a profound impact on mental health. However, by taking proactive steps such as seeking out new experiences, focusing on gratitude, building social connections, prioritizing self-care, and seeking out professional help when necessary, it is possible to regain a sense of purpose and find greater fulfillment in life. Remember that you are not alone, and there is always help available if you need it.